Sweetgrass
and Smoke

Sweetgrass and Smoke

Constance Cappel

Chapters I through X are a work of fiction. Names, characters,
places, and incidents are the product of the author's imagination
or are used fictitiously, and any resemblance to actual persons,
living or dead, business establishments, events, or locales is entirely
coincidental.

All permissions have been granted. C. Cappel took the cover
photographs of the Greensky Church from the site of Prudence
Bolton's grave and of Iris John at the Harbor Springs Pow-Wow in
2000.

This book was printed in the United States of America.

To order additional copies of this book, contact:
Xlibris Corporation
1-888-795-4274
www.Xlibris.com
Orders@Xlibris.com

Contents

"So that when you go in a place where Indians have lived you smell them gone and all the empty pain killer bottles and the flies that buzz do not kill the sweetgrass smell, the smoke smell and that other like a fresh cased marten skin."

"Fathers and Sons," *The Complete Short Stories of Ernest Hemingway: the Finca Vigia Edition.* P.375. New York: Charles Scribner's.

TO MY GRANDDAUGHTER,
AVERY GRACE MONTGOMERY

Preface

Ernest Hemingway was deeply influenced by his relationships with the Native Americans of northern Michigan. Thoughout his life he would refer to the many experiences that he had with the American Indians who were neighbors of the Hemingway family in northern Michigan. He hunted, fished, swapped tales, and had his first love affair with these Native American neigbors. He quickly incorporated these experiences into his early written work and continued to carry them in his memory. His oldest son, Jack Hemingway, told Candace Eaton, the director of the Little Traverse Historical Museum, in the autumn of 2000 that his father often told him stories about his life with the American Indians in northern Michigan. In his visit to the museum Jack Hemingway was particularly interested in the Native American exhibits.

The story of Ernest Hemingway and Prudence Bolton, his first love who was a Native American, has always haunted me, since I first heard about it in 1960 while researching my biography, *Hemingway in Michigan*. Ernest Hemingway's first relationship was one that he never forgot. Prudence Bolton kept appearing in his letters, fiction, and his thought during his whole life. She was the woman who, according to Hemingway, "did first what no one has done better." Of all of the incidents, which were included in *Hemingway in Michigan*, the one that people most frequently inquired about was that of Ernest, Prudence, and a possible child of theirs.

This book, *Sweetgrass and Smoke*, is an attempt to create in the printed form the story of Ernest and Prudence set in a historical, cultural, and a timeline experiment. In art it would be a collage, and in film it would be a documentary done with an MTV mix. Both fiction and non-fiction are woven together with the same theme using the voice of romantic fiction as the cornerstone of this book. Interspaced between the chapters of the novel is a mix of newspaper clippings, private letters, new interviews, Native American memoirs and legends, prehistory theories, and death notices. To the original blend of fact and fiction are woven entire chapters of my Hemingway biography, which sets the stage for new research and corrections in this book. Slicing between the spoken word, memoirs, public documents, new fiction, letters, and new interpretations, the past becomes present and the present past. This book is a postmodern, experimental, and multi-faceted document. It is a verbal collage of the truth, the possible truth, and the fictionalized truth woven into a historical, yet modern, tale.

Hemingway's portrayal of Prudence Bolton in his short stories, personal letters, and memory, as just a sex object is both demeaning and limited. She was a beautiful girl who died a tragic death at sixteen which makes her life story far deeper than that of the teenage rejection felt by Nick Adams in "Ten Indians" or the memorable sex described in "Fathers and Sons." A tragedy like Prudence's life and death is a more appropriate subject for *A Farewell to Arms,* and maybe it was the subconscious inspiration for that novel. His relationship with Agnes Kurowsky certainly did not end in her death or pregnancy.

Ernest Hemingway went to war immediately after he allegedly heard of Prudence's suicide. He was injured in World War I, but survived, and then returned to reside briefly in northern Michigan. His own suicide was not for forty-two more years. Prudence was ill used by two white men: Ernest Hemingway and then ultimately by Jim Castle, the man with whom she committed suicide. Jim Castle was a married man and criminal, who was recently released from jail and was awaiting sentencing for assault and robbery when he died. His female accomplice in the robbery had committed suicide in jail a few months before he convinced his new, live-in girlfriend, Prudence Bolton, to commit the same destiny with him on February 15, 1918. Prudence was supposedly several months pregnant when she died.

In the fall of 1991, I interviewed Jay Oliver, a Native American who knew Prudence Bolton, her family, and the Hemingway family. James Hartwell introduced me to Jay Oliver on the same day that he showed me Prudence's grave. Her unmarked grave was one of the mounds doted with haphazard crosses behind the one hundred and sixty year old Native American Greensky Church made of hand-hewn logs located on Susan Lake and pictured on the cover of this book. Prudence's dying cries over that same lake, as described in Peter Griffin's book, *Along With Youth,* were horrific. Driving the back dirt roads in the leafless woods near Walloon Lake, Horton Bay, and Lake Charlevoix in the autumn of 1991 was a haunting experience where I almost could feel the "Windigo" and other Native American spirits following me. I hurriedly drove out of northern Michigan in December of that year without a book written. I was glad to escape.

Several years later in the Peace Corps in Poland in 1993, I wrote the fictional part of this book. This hypothetical story is of an American Indian girl in the repressive Fifties who marries a wealthy, white man from Harbor Point, who is not a fictional Ernest Hemingway. But Hemingway's sexist and racist treatment of Prudence in his fiction and conversations throughout his life was always a wrong that seemed to need to be turned into a right, and this fictional story was a way to try a different viewpoint and outcome. Hemingway, as a white Englishman, carried on the exploitation of the Native Americans who had a tragic history in northern Michigan. Much of the Odawa nation was killed by a germ warfare (smallpox) trick described by Chief Blackbird in his book and included in *Sweetgrass and Smoke.* This incident in 1763 was the last use of biological warfare in the United States until the anthrax outbreak in 2001. Ernest Hemingway continued the colonial tradition by his treatment of not honoring a young neighbor who was a housekeeper/babysitter for his family. But what if a rich playboy, not Ernest Hemingway, wooed, honored, and married a young Native American from Harbor Springs? Having written the fictional part of *Sweetgrass and Smoke,* I put it into a drawer and forgot it.

Then in the summer of 2000, exactly forty years after the summer researching, *Hemingway in Michigan,* I found myself revisiting the old haunts (literally) and covering the same paths that I had traveled before. This time Prudence's death records in the Charlevoix County Courthouse jumped out at me from the handwritten entry in the record book. With the date of her death in hand I was able to track down the information of Prudence Bolton's death story as an unidentified "Indian girl" in the Petoskey paper. I had the facts, finally. The story of Prudence and Ernest and *Sweetgrass and Smoke* needed to be told. Their story was of two teenagers and first love. Fact and fiction, which could be which, is often overlapping in this work. This book becomes a puzzle within a puzzle within a maze. The tragic end and the suicides of Ernest and Prudence, decades apart, were of two former lovers who committed the same self-destructive act. Prudence died of strychnine poisoning as a teenager, violently and with extreme pain, crying out over the frozen wastes of the Susan Lake/Lake Charlevoix winter scene. Ernest Hemingway ended his action packed and famous life also in a violent suicide, but with a gun, on a summer morning in 1961 in Sun Valley, Idaho. Ernest and Prudence were two star-crossed lovers separated by different cultures and a lifetime, but they both choose to end their lives in suicide. Two tragedies, two suicides, and two cultures are the backbone and links in this book.

The help of many people in northern Michigan and elsewhere in the preparation of this book is appreciated. Jeff Brearley, Margie Bake, Betty Reddig, Bea MacGregor, Cheryl Choinski, Gloria Frank, Patsy Ketterer, and Pam and George Houk gave me important feedback about the Michigan accuracy in the novel part of *Sweetgrass and Smoke*. Michelle Schwartz did a fine job of typing the original manuscript. Iris John let me use her picture taken at the pow wow in Harbor Springs in August of 2000 for the cover of the book. Anson Montgomery gave valuable editorial and computer help to this project. My brother, Scott Cappel, gave many insights about the different versions of this book in its many stages and manifestations. This book is a result of a quest begun in the summer of 1960 in the forests and towns near Little Traverse Bay in northern Michigan and ending in the winter of 2002.

Constance Cappel, Ph.D.
Harbor Springs, Michigan
1960-2002

Introduction

My name is Crow Woman. I sing in the crying boughs of the Crooked Tree that my people could see as a marker from far off on the big lake, Lake Michigan. I am caught between earth and sky, neither up nor down, but always watching. All of my human kin have left earth, but I'm condemned in spirit form to wander my earthly haunts and trace the stories of my family, my American Indian tribe, the Wawgawnawkezee Odawas, the Little Traverse Bay Bands of Odawas.

Sad stories I watch and hear. Patterns repeating. This book is a chronicle of a lost soul, and of the story of her life and death. The Windigo follows her lamenting soul, ready to pounce. I protect her. Her name is Prudence Bolton.

She was a short time on earth in real time, just over sixteen years. Beautiful and strong, she attracted an Englishman who was to be a famous writer. Just as her ancestors were tricked and killed by the English, so was she. I watched her make love with this young man in the pine woods. I watched her initiate him into the secrets of love that would spoil him for the many white women that followed. He knew that she was the first and was the best. His name is Ernest Hemingway.

This man never gave her the trust and honor she deserved. He cared only for his ego and his pride. He never wrote about her character and how she died. He only wrote about his sexual fulfilliment with her.

Now I'm the trickster, as my name implies. What might happen, if the tables were turned? What if an Englishman married the Indian Princess? What if he loved her more than she loved him? What if the fairy tale worked out? So I whispered to the wind this story of a fictitious "Prudence Mitchell" with the same name that Ernest Hemingway gave Prudence Bolton in his fiction and played her against the real stories and the myths and the tales about my people and their life in northern Michigan. Now the reader can decide who is right and who is wrong and who is real and who is not.

Chapter I

SUMMER SOLSTICE

Trudy Mitchell leaned back into the mossy hillside and watched. She was good at watching and had spent most of her seventeen years doing just that. Her torso was twisted, so that she could rest on one arm while her hand ran between her legs and hooked beneath her folded leg that supported the one trailing off the soft mound under the bushes. She was barefoot.

No one knew where she was, and no one would know: this was her secret place. On the hill overgrown with sumac, birches, and maples, the wild roses were now in bloom. Trudy hung on a protected incline three-fourths the way up the bluff where the roses drenched her in their light perfume. An easy breeze came off the lake and mixed the rose perfume with that of the pine.

The summer solstice was today, and tonight the

sun would not set until almost ten. The afterglow
would be in the air until after eleven o'clock. Trudy
loved the changing seasons, but the longest day of
the year was her special day. She had always spent it
in her hiding place on the hillside, and last year she
brought along a blanket and pillow and spent the
night outside. No one knew that she was gone from
the house, and no one cared.

Now she warmed her legs in the sun and played
with a light pink rose. She smelled it and then put it
behind her ear like the Polynesian girls in Tahiti that
she read about in the *National Geographic* magazines
piled along with the hunting magazines in Curley's
Barber Shop. She loved to read and would read
anything. Curley teased her at first, but then he let
her come in the male domain, even when she was a
little girl, and sit among the men and read the gun
and car magazines. She would read the house and
garden and glossy social magazines at the summer
cottages on Harbor Point while babysitting there. Now
she was reading *The Rains Came* by Louis Bromfield
taken from the library. She liked Bromfield and
wanted to read all of his books this summer. After
she finished Bromfield, she planned to read the
Michigan short stories about Nick Adams that Ernest
Hemingway had written about her aunt, Prudence
Bolton. She had been named after the beautiful
Prudence, who had died tragically. Hemingway did
not change the names of many people in the
Michigan short stories or just changed their last name,
as he did with her aunt. He never thought that the
farmers and Indians would read his stories. But
Prudence loved to read. She loved the Harbor
Springs library on the second floor of the brick
building next to Hovey's drugstore. She would sit in

a comfortable chair and read while the smell of the cooking fudge in the shop below would waft up the stairs.

While she read and napped, an annoying sound kept bothering her. It was like a big mosquito that dive-bombs in a dark room at night and will not give you peace. She looked up through the prickly bushes protecting her outdoor room and looked out over the little town of Harbor Springs, over the deep water of the harbor to Harbor Point. The point jutted into the blue waters of Little Traverse Bay that protected Harbor Springs with the deepest natural harbor in the Great Lakes. Where was that sound coming from?

She slowly stood up, shaded her eyes, and looked from the glimmering horizon of the big lake, Lake Michigan, which stretched outward around the turn of the earth. Her gaze moved along the far shore of Little Traverse Bay from Charlevoix to Petoskey. Then she heard it coming closer, closing in over the trees behind her, dropping in the down draft of the bluff that backed the town, over her head, coming too close, then banking, a float plane, nicking the treetops, sputtering, and dropping onto the calm waters of the harbor. The plane taxied across the harbor and pulled up to the Little Harbor Club that was at the curve of land where the town met Harbor Point.

Trudy was glad that it had not crashed like she thought it might do. The summer people do crazy things, too, she thought, and yet they were always talking about "drunken Indians." She had seen as many drunken white people down at the Pier Bar as she had seen Indians.

Her peaceful afternoon was destroyed, and she decided to go over to her Aunt Alice's house. She folded up her blanket; the other half of her sandwich covered by wax paper and the bottle of Coke, and stuffed them in her woven bag with the quill design that her mother made. She tucked her Louis Bromfield book about the other Indians on the other side of the world into it on the nonfood side.

Aunt Alice should be holding court about now, she thought, as she walked by all of the big houses on the bluff overlooking the lake. She knew every family, knew who owned every house, and knew when to look at the sidewalk and when to look up at the people sitting on the porches. The cool breeze cut the hottest part of the day, and everyone was taking advantage of it on their porch.

Aunt Alice's house was not on the bluff, but on a side street, which ran up an incline. Her house was neat and clean and freshly painted, but not anything like the big houses. Trudy liked it better. Some of the bluff big houses had dark wood inside or were made of stone, so that they were cold and damp even on a warm summer day like today. Aunt Alice's little frame house with the peaked roof and the sweet smelling freshly cut front lawn was much more preferable to Trudy. "What do you do with all of those empty rooms in a big house?" she thought.

Alice Mitchell was on the white side of Trudy's family, married to her father's brother, and came from one of the families that had settled the town. Alice had always had a soft spot for her no-good brother-in-law's oldest daughter. Dick Mitchell was a disgrace to the Mitchell family. He was a drunken bum, Aunt Alice would tell the ladies who congregated at her house, and he lived in a common law marriage in a shack in Indian town with Trudy's mother who was a Tabeshaw. Why Irene Tabeshaw put up with Dick Mitchell, she never knew. "Maybe because she was a squaw and one of the crazy drunken Tabashaws, Irene never knew any better," thought Alice.

When Trudy came up her aunt's well-swept concrete walk, Alice greeted her at the door.

"Look what the cat dragged in," she announced Trudy to the two other women sitting on her porch. "Where have you been, child? Your hair's a mess."

Trudy ran her hand over her hair and pulled out a tangled thorn branch from the wild rose bush. She just smiled at her Aunt Alice and the other women.

"Well, don't just stand there, barefoot and all. Come on up and have some lemonade."

Trudy looked down and shyly sat on the step below the women. That is why they liked Dick Mitchell's daughter; she knew her place and never put on any airs. Trudy learned early to talk to white people in monosyllables and look downward. Only in her writing and by herself could she verbalize the difficult syntax and the rhythms of the writers she read.

Mrs. Herbert leaned over when Alice left the porch and asked Trudy, if she had any shoes. Trudy pulled a pair out of her basket and then put them back in.

"Well, Trudy, here's some cool lemonade on this hot afternoon." Alice never walked, she bustled. She gave Trudy a glass and at the same time pulled the wild rose from behind her ear and threw it away. "Where are your shoes?"

Trudy again pulled them out of her bag and put them back in.

"Now, Trudy, you know young ladies should wear shoes. You aren't a little girl now."

Trudy put on her shoes.

"Emma, did you hear about what happened to Judge Harris at the barber shop the other day?" Alice began a long, humorous story about the pompous Judge Harris, and Trudy became her invisible self. Sometimes she would be invisible for hours, sometimes days, just taking up space and watching and listening, but not being seen or heard. At this moment she became part of the white pillar holding up the porch. She could hear the women talk about the people in the town. She could feel the lake breeze on her sweaty, sunburnt arm, but no one saw her. Aunt Alice let her listen to grown-up talk even when she was a small girl. Now she knew all of the interweaving of the people in town, both in Indian town and among the white folks. If she was quiet and didn't ask questions, she was allowed to listen and learn.

Trudy learned. Trudy learned that Indians were worthless. Trudy learned that the Tabashaws wouldn't do a decent day's work. Prudence Mitchell learned that even though she went to the white high school and got good grades that she would always be Dick Mitchell's out-of-wedlock half-breed daughter.

She leaned over and picked the scab on her knee.

"Trudy, don't do that. You'll infect it," said Mrs. Henshaw, the doctor's wife.

"I stopped the bleeding," she said.

"I can see that. Did you put mercurochrome on it?"

"No, I put spider webs on it."

"My heavens, girl, I'm surprised you aren't infected now."

"Stops the bleeding," Trudy whispered.

"Who told you that?" Mrs. Henshaw straightened

her already straight back.

"My mother," Trudy whispered.

"Now Doris," Alice said, "Trudy has her own ways."

They gave each other that look Trudy had seen many times. "But the real question is whether you are going to help me with the lemonade and cookies after church on Sunday, Trudy?"

All the women turned and smiled now at Trudy, because she went to the Methodist Church with her Aunt Alice instead of the Catholic Church with the Indians. Alice, who was a dressmaker, had always made nice dresses for Trudy to wear on Sunday when she went to church with the two other women on the porch. They knew that she was different than many of the other teenagers in town who were hung over on Sunday and didn't go to church. She was certainly different than her parents.

The telephone rang, and Alice went inside to answer it. Trudy gazed at the harbor and thought of the floatplane gradually lifting off the water. The other two women talked among themselves. The breeze died down and a heavy four o'clock in the afternoon warmth settled over the town. Soon the water would be glassy smooth in the harbor by the time the six o'clock church bells rang simultaneously in the bell towers of the five churches. Harbor Springs was like an English village at six a.m., noon, and six p.m. with the ringing choir of church bells pealing in the quiet air.

Alice hurried back onto the porch with a fresh batch of chocolate chip cookies and another pitcher of lemonade. She was known for her hospitality and especially her Sunday suppers when friends just dropped by. Trudy let the warm cookies dissolve in her mouth with the chocolate chips slowly melting and then washed them down with the ice-cold lemonade.

"That was Mrs. George Fay," said Alice, as she settled into her chair after serving her guests and Trudy. She always called her clients by their full, married names when she spoke about them to the townspeople. She felt that they should be given the respect that their wealth and social position afforded them. The other two women leaned forward, because Mrs. Fay was the top of the social ladder on Harbor Point with the biggest summer cottage. The Fay's one hundred foot yacht always told the townspeople that the summer season had begun. When "Fay's Folly" rounded the end of the Point on it's return from Florida, they knew that all of the other yachts were on their way up the intercoastal waterway on the Atlantic coast or were heading down the St. Lawrence towards the Great Lakes.

"Mrs. George Fay," she began again for emphasis, "Needs her coral chiffon for the Saturday night dance at the Little Harbor Club tonight. She was going to wear her navy blue satin, but felt that it was too wintery for such a summery day. Luckily, I just finished the chiffon before you came. Do you want to see it?" The two women nodded in unison.

"Here it is!" Alice held up the cocktail dress made of layers of chiffon, which would cover Mrs. George Fay's bulk in flattering effects of optical illusions. "I know that it cost five hundred, if it cost a penny. It has a label from New York, Cassini something." She held the dress closer, so that the two women could finger the cloth.

When she took the dress inside, the two women whispered to each other, so that Trudy and her aunt would not hear.

"I wonder if the high-faluting Mrs. George Fay knows what her three daughters are up to?"

"No? What?"

"Well, Billy at the grocery store says while their mother is playing cards in the afternoon and their father is playing golf, they have young gentlemen over to the house."

"So what, that isn't . . ."

"No. It's not just entertaining them. Billy was delivering groceries one afternoon and when he came up on the back porch, all of the window blinds were pulled down."

"Yes?"

"Well, he didn't think anyone was home, so he brought the groceries right into the kitchen. He heard something in the darkened living room. The two older daughters were stark naked with two young men on the floor. Now, get this, the youngest was sitting on the couch fully dressed watching them."

"No!"

"Yes, Billy told my son, Evett, swore on the Bible."

"The youngest one is only fourteen, or the most fifteen."

"That's right."

Alice came back with a dress box carefully wrapped.

"Trudy are you doing anything?" She asked.

"No. Not much."

"Then you can drop Mrs. Fay's dress off when you go home."

"I can't go out on the Point."

"I know, I know," Alice knew the rules. "Just leave it with the guard at the gate, and Mrs. Fay will have someone pick it up."

Trudy felt ready to go anyway, since she usually

headed home at dinner to help her mother through the chaos of dealing with a baby, a toddler, an eight-year old angry boy, and a usually drunken husband. There would have been more children, but Dick Mitchell was gone for eight years in Alaska after Trudy was born. Her mother lost two children.

Alice carefully gave her the box with instructions of how to carry it and what to do with it. Trudy seriously took it from her and gingerly held it, as she slowly went down the walk. What Alice and her two friends, who went back to their gossip as soon as Trudy left, did not see was what Trudy did when she rounded the corner and was out of sight. She put the box down on the grass, kicked her shoes off and put them in her basket, picked another wild rose from a bush at the top of the bluff to put in her hair, and then haphazardly held the box under her arm, as she ran full tilt down the zigzag path of the steep bluff.

Trudy felt her heels dig into the sandy earth, hopped over tree roots that tripped up others, leaned under the clothes line at the bottom of the hill that toppled drunks coming home in the dark, ran across the yards on the well-worn path, and out on the street near the little Episcopal Church that was only open in the summer. She noticed that it was freshly painted and the front door was open, so that it was ready for the summer folks. Then she moved quickly past the dusty playground near the Catholic Church where all the Indian children were playing under the eyes of the nuns. The sisters ran a boarding school year around, and some of the children had not been with their parents in a long time. Her feet were counting the cracks in the uneven sidewalk, as she moved beyond the end of

Main Street and headed past the Little Harbor Club
with its "Members Only" sign.

Trudy paused, hidden by the pines, to look in at
the bluest-of-all swimming pools and the summer
people dressed in white clothes playing tennis. They
always seemed to be laughing and happy. She
watched a couple that were sitting and watching the
tennis players while drinking their cocktails. The
woman seemed no older than she was. She had blond
hair and wore a white tennis dress.

Trudy looked down at her own bare feet, year
around bronze skin, her dark blue short shorts, not
the longer Bermuda shorts worn by the women at
the club, and she felt that she was the outsider. These
people invaded her town every summer, but she felt
that they owned it, not her. She was like the rest of
the townspeople who were expected to wait on them
for the summer and then to sink into oblivion for
the other nine months of the year. Sometimes this
life of hers made her mad, and she wanted to make
everything right and fair for herself and her loved
ones in one bold stroke.

But what chance did she have? She would be
lucky, if she could scrape together enough money to
go down state to a second-rate college. She had been
the valedictorian at graduation from Harbor Springs
High School and won a scholarship, but it was only
$300. The teenagers, whose families lived on the
bluff, were going to the University of Michigan at
Ann Arbor where their parents had gone, even
though their grades were not as good as Trudy's.
When Trudy asked Mr. Ross, the guidance counselor
about this, he told her that even if she had all the
money needed that the other students had a better
chance than she did, and especially the boys who

were good athletes. Mr. Ross then suggested a two-year college where one Indian girl had gone several years before. Trudy never asked him for his advice again, and now she had no plans for the fall semester. All of the catalogs, which she had excitedly sent away for in her junior year, lay in a corner of her bedroom.

Trudy snapped out of her daydreaming and watching the people like she remembered Jay Gatsby doing in F. Scott Fitzgerald's book. People were always making fun of her when she compared herself to the characters in the books she read, especially when she compared herself to the heroes, the main characters, not the women who were supporting characters in the novels. Even the librarian at the Harbor Springs library told her, when Trudy tried to talk to her about the interesting people she was reading about, to "read more Nancy Drew, not all of the grown-up books." Trudy told her that she had already read all of the Nancy Drew books.

With the late afternoon sun coming through the full-leafed maples shielding the street, Trudy continued barefoot to the entrance of "The Point." A rounded gateway made partially of stone rose up over the road while the public road turned to follow the shoreline. Indian legend had this place between the point of land jutting out into the lake and the mainland as a sacred place where the white men had filled in a small sacred pond inhabited by a spirit when they built their summer cottages on what they called "Harbor Point." Now Trudy or any other Indian was barred from their former sacred land. They were allowed out on the Point only as servants, delivery people, or gardeners. Even then they were questioned and treated rudely by the guards at the gate.

When Trudy approached the gate which said: "Harbor Point Association" with a smaller sign "Private Property" underneath it, she had that nervous feeling she always had near the Point. She quickly put on her shoes and wondered, if she looked "ladylike" enough. She forgot the wild rose in her hair. She straightened her white cotton blouse and tucked it in and pulled her blue cotton shorts down to cover more of her legs.

Luckily, Teddy Barns, who was three years ahead of her at the high school, was one of the security guards on duty. He had always liked her and once took her to a football game. He now had her sit on the bench with the two colored maids while he called the Fay cottage. Teddy told Trudy to wait, and someone would soon be down to pick up the dress.

Trudy became invisible against the cold, stone wall and waited next to the chatting maids.

Chapter A

Background material
From *Michigan Prehistory Mysteries,*
Betty Sodders, Avery Color Studios,
Au Train, Michigan, 1990, pp, 82-85.

The Stonehenge ruins were immense, the Beaver Island finds. Much smaller in scope but nevertheless important. If, as believed, the stones offered the ancients a form of calendar, it would be evident to their very existence. There has been speculation the ring of stones allowed not only tracking of the sun, but determining the seasons as well.

*   *   *

It is accepted fact that stone rings and related rock monuments outcropped from the megalithic era. It is also known that there is a definite connection to edifices such as Stonehenge between these ringed structures and astronomical science. One of the best-known sites here in North America is located at Mystery Hill, North Salem, New Hampshire. Here is found a stone chamber observatory together with a stone circle. (The chamber bears resemblance to the astroalignment pits of Isle Royal, while the stone circle relates to the Beaver Island "ring of stones".) At the Mystery Hill site, brush and debris was cleared, revealing that one stone marks the meridian and lies due north of the central observation point. Four other rocks indicate the sunrise and sunset points on the horizon for the midsummer and midwinter solstices.

All across the United States stone circles have been found, varying in size from small to large. Many contain massive boulders up to, say, 15 meters in circumference, involving great labor to merely position them properly.

Understanding just how stone circles and other forms of crude megalithic observatories work is important. During the course of a 12-month period, the sun moves across the horizon, a short measured distance each day. On the first day of spring (March 21), and autumn (September 21) the vernal equinox and the autumnal equinox, the sun rises due east and sets due west. With the approach of the summer equinox (June 21), the sun's northward

journey comes to a slow stop and from that
time on the process reverses. Half a year
later the winter solstice (December 21),
signals the reversal once again. The year is
so completed. You can readily see the
solstices are very important quarter-way
marks along the equinox system. The
results of the whole system might be that
should a person place an object on the
ground, lined up with a second, the
shadows will indicate a functional guide if
properly aligned. Once the two solstices are
plotted out by a permanent marker, other
points can then comprise the solar calendar.

Archaeologists maintain the axis of the
Beaver Island "circle of stones" is aligned
approximately on the point of the
midsummer sunrise, and is believed to have
been constructed by a cult of ancient sun
worshippers or for use as a calendar.

This evidence of ancient man's
endeavor was found on the west central side
of this 53-square-mile island northwest of
Charlevoix on the mainland. The circular
structure is made up of 39 stones forming a
397-foot circle. Stones vary sizewise from 2
feet to 10 feet in diameter. Experts say the
boulders are placed horizontally rather than
upright. The center rock that occupies the
middle position of the boulders contains a
hole the size of a basketball, believed to have
been chiseled by humans. Speculation
indicates it may have once held a pole,
probably serving in the capacity of a sundial.
Furthermore, authorities attribute this rock

circle to be man-made since there is little evidence of other boulders of that size-range in the immediate area.

This incomprehensible stone circle was first discovered in the summer of 1985 by Terri Bussey while searching for Indian artifacts. According to George Weeks, Staff Writer for the Detroit News, "Bussey came upon a large boulder on the west end of the island. The top of the rock had a large hole. Bussey remarked it resembled any other rock with a hole in it. But on closer examination she became convinced the hole had been chiseled out and the rock had what appeared to be a man-made grid."

Weeks continues, "To check out a suspicion she had about its significance, she paced off from the rock to points of the compass, where she found more large stones, mostly buried. She charted the sunrise and sunset over certain rocks. For two nights she camped in the area noting alignment of the stars."

It should be stated here that Terri Bussey is part Chippewa and presently is the director of the Grand Rapids Inter-Tribal Council's Michigan Indian Press. Excited over her discovery, she took her findings to members of the Grand Traverse Band of Ottawa and Chippewa Indians. She also tried to interest archaeologists in excavating near the site.

But based on what was previously known about prehistory culture in the Beaver Island area, archaeologists remarked that it

would make little sense to suspect there
would be anything resembling a "mini-
Stonehenge" on the island.

Newspaper accounts, however, relate
Dr. Donald P. Heldman, archaeologist in
charge of excavations at Fort Michilimackinac
at Mackinaw City, was intrigued. He made a
trip out to the island, met with Ms. Bussey,
and after preliminary examinations,
determined Bussey had indeed discovered
a circle of boulders placed by human hands.
Since Heldman's initial findings, Bussey
has had aerial photographs taken of the site
with infrared film; however, results are not
yet confirmed.

Once again, a similar question
interjected in other chapters of this book,
takes center stage. Who made this
megalithic calendar from the far distant
past? We have already discussed the
inherent possibility the early primitive
inhabitants may have stemmed from Celtic
or Norse heritage. So in turn, let's explore
two other avenues of thought.

Many archaeologists attribute both the
mounds and stone rings to the people of
the Mississippian culture . . . The Mound-
Builders. It is reported their civilization
stretched from Lake Superior to the Gulf
of Mexico and from the Mississippi River to
the Carolinas. In the chronology of the
Upper Midwest, the Mississippians arrived
in Michigan relatively late, about 1200 A.D.,
although they existed much earlier to the
south of us. Several distinct periods mark

this era: Emergent Mississippian, 800-1000
A.D.; Early Woodland, 950-1050 A.D.;
Middle Woodland, 1050-1300 A.D.; and
finally the Late Woodland period, 1350-
1541 A.D.

During the phase termed the Early
Woodland Period, the Mississippians
founded the town of Cahokia, near St. Louis,
Missouri. It proved to be a major metropolis,
a political and ceremonial center that grew
in size to 6 square miles, with an estimated
population near 40,000 inhabitants.

As time marched on, the middle phase
of this culture group expanded into the
Great Lakes region. Here their largest city
was named Aztalan, located in present-day
southeastern Wisconsin. Historians and
scientists alike speculate this too was a way-
station for transporting natural resources
such as copper and animal skins to other
Mississippian villages further south. It is
indeed interesting to note that artifacts
found at both the Wisconsin site and the
location in St. Louis interrelate.

*   *   *

History of the Ottawa
and Chippewa Indians of Michigan,
Andrew S. Blackbird, published 1887,
reprinted by the
Little Traverse Historical Society,
Petoskey, Michigan, pp.11-12.

In my first recollection of the country

of Arbor Croche, (*The word Arbor Croche is derived from two French words: Arbre, a tree; and Croche, something very crooked or hook-like. The tradition says when the Ottawas first came to that part of the country a great pine tree stood very near the shore where Middle Village now is, whose top was very crooked, almost hook-like. Therefore the Ottawas called the place "Wau-gaw-naw-ke-zee"— meaning the crooked top of the tree. But by and by the whole coast from Little Traverse to Tehin-gaw-beng, now Cross Village, became denominated as Wau-gaw-naw-ke-zee.*) which is sixty years ago, there was nothing but small shrubbery here and there in small patches, such as wild cherry trees, but the most of it was grassy plain; and such an abundance of wild strawberries, raspberries and blackberries that they fairly perfumed the air of the whole coast with fragrant scent of ripe fruit. The wild pigeons and every variety of feathered songsters filled all the groves, warbling their songs joyfully and feasting upon these wild fruits of nature; and in these waters the fishes were so plentiful that as you lift up the anchor-stone of your net in the morning, your net would be so loaded with delicious whitefish as to fairly float with all its weight of the sinkers. As you look towards the course of your net, you see the fins of the fishes sticking out of the water in every way. Then I never knew my people to want for anything to eat or to wear, as we always had plenty of wild meat and plenty of fish, corn, vegetables, and wild fruits. I thought (and yet I may be mistaken) that my people were very happy in those days, at least I was as happy myself as a lark, or as the brown thrush that sat daily on the uppermost branches of the stubby growth of a basswood tree which stood near by upon the hill where we often played under its shade, lodging our little arrows among the thick branches of the tree and then shooting them down again for sport.

Early in the morning as the sun peeped from the east, as I would yet be lying close to my mother's bosom, this brown thrush would begin his warbling songs perched upon the uppermost branches of the basswood tree that stood close to our lodge. I would then say to myself, as I listened to him, "here comes again my little orator," and I used to try to understand what he had to say; and sometimes thought I understood some of its utterances as follows: "Good morning, good morning! Arise, arise! Shoot, shoot! Come along, come along!" Etc., every word repeated twice. Even then, and so young as I was, I used to think that little bird had a language which God or the Great Spirit had given him, and every bird of the forest understood what he had to say, and that he was appointed to preach to other birds, to tell them to be happy, to be thankful for the blessings they enjoy among the summer green branches of the forest, and the plenty of wild fruits to eat. The larger boys used to amuse themselves by playing a ball called Paw-kaw-do-way, foot-racing, wrestling, bow-arrow shooting, and trying to

beat one another shooting the greatest
number of chipmunks and squirrels in a
day, etc.

From *Ancient Mines of Kitchi-Gummi: A Case Study*, Roger Jewell, Jewell Histories, Fairfield, PA, 2000, pp. 98-99.

This critical religious and secular information was so important in the everyday
lives of these people; it could not be left to
memory alone. The exact days of the winter
solstice, the equinox, summer solstice, and
fall equinox were very important. These
annual cycles or rhythms gave meaning and
balance to the daily work of these cultures.
This was the reason for the use of circles—
first Woodhenge, then Stonehenge. What
better display of Father Sun's faithful returning cycle, then his re-appearance each
year exactly as predicted by the religious
leaders.

Like their sun alters, the monolith us-
ers came to depend on large stones to mark
other important places, for example, the
burial places of important leaders. Even
when they moved into the more specialized
professions like traders, or metal workers,
their Sun God symbols were taken along.
They set them up at their seasonal outposts.
Eventually, we have equinox marks and calendar sites far from the farm-based Neolithic
centers. It is obvious that they are no longer

used as important secular calendars, but they are now part of the religious and spiritual ceremonies.

It is for this reason, I believe, that we find calendar sites, dolmens, and standing stones in the rocky Laurention Shield country of Ontario, Canada, and in some of the northern lake states like Minnesota and Michigan. This country was not used for farming. The only real remaining reason being here was for the mining of copper, silver, and gold.

Chapter II

ERNEST BARKER WOODWARD, III

Woody dropped the plane over the trees searching for the down draft. He could feel the invisible currents of air like a blind man. He knew where the air lifted off the water, pushed against the bluff, and sunk again. Fingering the throttle gently and banking the plane slowly, he cut the engine. No one in their right mind would deliberately do such a thing. Woody did.

The girl riding in the co-pilot's seat screamed. Woody smiled and eased the plane over the telephone wires without power. She grabbed on his arm and went pale under her tan. He pulled at the choke and started the plane up again, just as it skirted the downtown buildings of Harbor Springs. Her fingernails were hurting his arm. Woody shrugged her off and settled the floatplane between two moored sailboats and taxied it among jubilant speedboats with water skiers behind them. He coasted up to the dock at the Little Harbor Club.

Bitsy Fay felt like throwing up. When they landed, she scrambled out of the plane and onto the dock. A crowd had assembled, and Woody secured the plane, as Bitsy ran to the downstairs powder room of the club. All of the young people and a few of their parents were talking at once and asking Woody questions. He looked bored, as he walked towards the bar.

Ernest Barker Woodward, III was the heir to a large automotive fortune. Not content with the debutante parties and social constraints of Grosse Pointe, he had struggled through one year of General Studies at Columbia after barely graduating from Avon Old Farms. Studying was not his forte, nor was a desk job. Woody's father had died when he was fourteen, and his mother was on her third husband.

"Buy ya a drink," Mr. Pierce, who was head of the largest bank in Louisville, said to Woody, as he slapped him across the narrow of his back. Woody kept walking towards the bar, Mr. Pierce admired the young man who went his own way and did not run with the pack at the Little Harbor Club.

"Okay, just one. I must get the plane over to its mooring in one piece."

"Wonder if the harbor patrol could arrest you for drunken driving on a float plane?"

"I don't know, but I don't want to test them. It's one thing to get a citation in the speed boat and another to mess up my pilot's license."

Woody dropped in a chair on the terrace and stretched his legs under a table with the umbrella over it. Mr. Pierce pulled up a chair and waved for the waiter.

"Two bourbons and branch water here. That okay, son?"

Woody said, "Make mine soda," then nodded, took his aviator glasses off, and rubbed his bloodshot eyes, "Hair of the dog, last night was a rough one."

Mr. Pierce laughed. He knew Woody and the Fay girls had closed the bar last night. As president of the club he made it a point to know such things.

"Bitsy Fay is a cute, little thing, isn't she?" Mr. Pierce asked.

Woody took a sip of the drink and let the soda fizzle the bourbon to the back of his mouth. "Uh-huh," he nodded.

"Little young for you though?"

"Uh-huh."

"What are you now, son?"

"Twenty-five."

"Really. Only twenty-five. I'd guessed thirty or thirty-five."

"I look that frazzled?"

"No, but you flew in the Berlin airlift?"

"Uh-huh."

Bitsy appeared, and Woody was glad to see her. He wanted to get away from the old duffer. He was nervous.

"Let's go upstairs." Woody stood up. "I have to settle my monthly bar tab. Excuse us, Mr. Pierce, and thanks for the drink."

"Anytime. Anytime. My pleasure." Ambrose Pierce was disappointed. He wanted to hear more about the young man's adventures.

Bitsy was smiling, as she led Woody away from the other girls on the terrace. She had landed the catch of the season, and she was not going to let them forget it. She waved from the stairs leading to the second floor balcony, as she went hand in hand with Woody. At the top of the stairs he extracted his hand from her tight grip and wiped it on his khaki shorts. Her hand was clammy for such a hot day, he thought. Then he remembered her naked body beneath him, and thought that she's always a little clammy.

Woody was getting uneasy about her. The guys who spent their afternoons at the club bar considered her and her sister nymphos. One afternoon when he was drunk, Bitsy and her sister, Sudsy, had invited Emmet Thurston and himself over to their cottage on the Point to play cards. The card game turned out to be strip poker, and the next thing he realized that he was on the floor with all his clothes off with Bitsy flat on her back, not moving a muscle, in the missionary position. She was very proud of herself for giving herself to him and was not the least bit upset by her sister and Emmet next to them doing the same thing while their younger sister watched.

Woody had avoided her for a week after that. Then he weakened on another night and took her home in the speedboat and again was with her on the cold, sticky night. He looked at her now, so proud to be leading him away from the group on the terrace. She and her sister were the two most popular girls at the club. The other girls envied their blonde pageboys, their tanned, trim figures, and their daddy's fortune. They reminded Woody of red-eyed white rabbits, weak and not very smart.

"Woody, dear, I'll go out by the swimming pool and save us a table while you pay your bill," Bitsy said, as she went through the screen doors out to the pool built above the tennis courts. She was wearing her white tennis dress from her morning lesson. Bitsy wore her tennis dress all day, because the white showed off her tan, and the short skirt showed off her legs. She knew that she looked good today.

As she sunk into a meshed chair and ordered a drink from one of the college students who worked as waiters and waitresses at the club, she thought about Woody. That spring she had broken up with one of the wealthiest young men on the East Coast. Her mother was devastated, since she had planned the whole wedding and the reception following at the Saint Louis Country Club in her mind. Bitsy felt like a failure, since she had not gotten her "ring by spring" like most of her other classmates at Briarcliff Junior College. Here she was already nineteen and ready to be "put on the shelf" one year after she came out in St. Louis at the Veiled Prophet Ball.

But who had been dropped into her lap, but the mysterious Woody Woodward. She had heard about his exploits for years, but had not seen him, since she was a thirteen year old with braces. He was that much older than her, seeming dangerous and exciting, not like the boys her age. And her mother approved.

Woody came through the screened doors looking tan and lean. His curly light-brown hair was closely cropped, and his face was well proportioned, not handsome, but interesting. The most remarkable feature about Woody, were his eyes when he took off his sunglasses. They were gray, wild wolf's eyes. He was not a domesticated animal, but one that kept his distance and kept his own company. He did not trust anybody and always sat with his back against the wall.

Woody edged into the seat next to Bitsy, and

asked, "Did you order?"

"Yes, dear, another bourbon and soda," she reached across the table and touched the back of his hand. Her charm bracelet jangled on the metal table.

Woody pulled his hand away and clasped both hands behind his head.

Bitsy had a mission. Woody had not directly asked her to the big dance tonight, although she had dropped hints all week.

"Woody, are you taking your speed boat tonight?"

"Where?"

"To the dance at the Club."

"Maybe. Maybe not."

"I don't mind wearing my red dress in a speedboat."

"Maybe I'll just go down to the Pier Bar and get smashed with the Indians."

Bitsy hated this common element in Woody, but at the same time it made him more alluring. He was not afraid to go into any bar in northern Michigan.

"Well, we could go to the Pier after the Club . . ."

"But maybe I'll go to the VFW."

Bitsy was silent. No women were allowed inside, and no one she knew had ever gone into the corner building in town.

The waiter returned with their drinks. After he served them, he gave Bitsy a message.

"Oh, Woody. It's from Mummy. She needs to have some stupid dress picked up at the Harbor Point gate, and I have to run into town to pick up a prescription at the drugstore now. Could you pick it up on the way home?"

"Sure." Woody was staring through the people playing tennis.

"What a darling." She arose and gave him a peck

on the head. "And by the way, she's made reservations
for the two of us at dinner tonight at the family table."
She was walking away and hoped he wouldn't say
"no." When he was silent, she turned and said, "Seven
at the club. On the terrace, I think." She left quickly
before he could respond.

Woody sat looking at the tennis players. He was
beginning to feel anxious. Now he had to pick up
some dress, get the plane back to its mooring, and
be seen by everyone on a Saturday night at the Fay
table. The next thing he would know they would be
announcing his engagement while he had his mouth
full and could not answer.

"Oh, well, let's get the worst thing over first," he
thought. "Pick up the dress." He pulled himself to
his feet, walked down the concrete steps past the
tennis courts, and went onto the sidewalk past the
giant willow, which lead to the Point.

He crossed the broad, manicured lawn, which
ran into the harbor and walked up to the guards at
the gate.

"I'm here to pick up Mrs. Fay's dress." They
nodded toward the three women sitting in the
shadow of the entryway.

Woody saw two women in uniform and next to
them was sitting May Ling with a box on her lap. He
stared into the gloom. She did not disappear. He
stood still, rubbed his eyes after he took off his glasses,
and looked again. The girl looked back at him. He
felt strange, as if he were lifting up. Maybe it was the
two drinks on an empty stomach. May Ling could
not be sitting here on the bench. She was still in
Thailand. Or he thought she was. She smiled at him
and stood up holding the box.

"Mrs. Fay's dress?" he asked.

"Mrs. Fay's dress," she answered in perfect English with no accent.

"Who are you?"

"Trudy Mitchell."

"Trudy Mitchell? Where do you live?"

"Harbor." She was not going to tell him Indian town.

"How long have you lived here?"

"Seventeen years."

"Seventeen years. Are you seventeen?"

"Yes." He was making her uncomfortable the way he kept staring at her, as if she would disappear. "Here is the dress." She handed it to him, but he was acting strange, just looking at her through his squinting wolf eyes. She turned to go.

"No, you can't leave again."

"I must go," she turned. He reached out and grabbed her arm. Now she got a wild look in her eyes, as she tried to pull loose.

"Please, please, stay just a minute." He held on to her warm bronze arm that clutched an Indian basket. "Who are you?"

"I told you that I'm Trudy Mitchell," she was beginning to be frightened and looked over at Teddy Barns who was watching them. "Please, let me go."

He looked down at his hand, as if it belonged to someone else. "Oh, I'm sorry. I thought you were someone else." He released her arm just as Teddy Barns strolled up.

"Problem here?" Teddy looked at Trudy.

"No, it's okay," she said, as she rubbed her arm, which was still encircled by a lighter shade where Woody had grasped her. She turned and walked quickly out of the gate and down the street.

Woody stared at her as she disappeared into the bushes across the street from the Club.

*   *   *

Woody had gone to Bangkok for some R&R after flying for two weeks straight. When they hit town, he and his buddy went straight to the red light district. Bangkok was wide open and anything that a rich man wanted he could get. They went into several clubs and were jostled by Thai women as soon as they crossed the threshold. Woody's friend, George, had been around the bars and yelled a foul word in Thai that made the women fall back, as if they had been kicked. The two men watched the two young women on stage do things that they did not think possible.

Later in the evening they went into the Red Dragon when it had reached a fever pitch. Tiny little Thai girls in their early teens sat on the laps of large white men with big noses at the bar. Woody and George sat in the corner where Woody could wedge his back against the wall and survey the room. He had a knife on one leg and a gun on the other. They ordered drinks and surveyed the crowd. Bar girls crept up to them chattering and slipped their hands in their laps. Smoke was thick and the American love songs were echoing in the heavy air.

A line of new prospects came out on the curved runway above the bar. The lead girl was confident and girls were copying her and trying to be just as alluring and desirable. Only one girl was different. She hung back and tried to cover her body rather than expose it. Instead of looking at the men watching her with the dead snake eyes of the lead

girl, she looked at the floor, the mirrored ceiling,
anywhere but into the men's eyes.

"Hey, what about the girl on the end?" Woody
asked his buddy.

"Not my type. Acts too much like my sister."

"No. Not for you."

"What do you mean?"

"I mean I want her. What do I do?"

"Go up to the bartender and pay for her."

"Okay." Woody went to the bartender, who made
the transaction in English, and then pulled the girl
from the platform. She lead Woody to a sweet-
smelling room in the back that had a large round
tub in it and a bed on a wooden platform.

"What's your name?"

"May Ling." She still had not looked at him, but
gently began taking his clothes off and folding them
neatly in a pile next to the bed.

"May Ling, that's a nice name."

She continued her assigned task methodically and
efficiently.

"May Ling, why don't you sit down and just talk a
little."

She sat obediently on the bed with her hands
folded between her legs.

"May Ling," Woody liked saying her name already,
"Where are you from?"

"South. Kok Sumui."

"I hear that's a beautiful island. Do you miss your
home?"

She looked away from him and stood up.

He also stood up to see her face.

"Into tub. Must take bubble bath," she said, as
she continued to undress him.

When he was in the tub, she gently washed him,

as a mother would wash her baby. She toweled him dry, made him lie on the bed, and applied scented oil on his tired back. He dozed off under her firm hands that erased all of the tension of the flying and round-the-clock duty. She then rolled him over and began arousing him. She dropped her silk dress and climbed up to work on him.

He pulled her down and began to try to give her some pleasure.

"No. Me do to you."

"But I want to. I want to make you happy," he said.

"No, me make you happy."

"Why?"

"My job."

"Just your job?"

"You pay. Me make you happy."

Woody sat up and pulled the silk sheet around him. May Ling still had not looked at him, as she lay naked beside him.

"Have you done this before?"

"Three times before."

"Come on. We are getting out of here."

Woody dragged May Ling to the bartender and told him that he was taking her to his hotel. The bartender gleefully transferred her hourly rate into a twenty-four hour rate, padded Woody's drink bill, and took the equivalent of ten girls' work for the evening. He was pleased with this transaction.

May Ling was crying when Woody pulled her into a motorized rickshaw with him. She was shaking and sobbing by the time they got to the hotel. He put his coat around her as he hurried her to the elevator. Her feet were barely touching the ground in the three inch sling back heels that were designed to throw her small breasts forward and make her backside seem fuller and ready for mounting. She was packaged and designed as an Oriental woman for a Western market. Woody pulled her into the hotel room, locked the door, and turned on the lights. The mildew smell seeped through the disinfectant used by the hotel. The air-conditioner choked and wheezed exchanging the cigar smell in the room for the dark polluted smell of nearby canals.

Woody put out two glasses and filled them with some Bourbon he had brought with him. He drank his neat and looked at May Ling sobbing and looking like a little toy doll sitting on the chair.

"Bottom's up," he handed her the glass and poured himself another.

She pretended to drink it, but went to the bathroom and poured it down the sink.

"Come on. Have a drink. It will help," he pleaded.

"No help. You no beat me?"

"Beat you? Why would I beat you?"

"Men pay for night. Take me to hotel. Beat me."

"Oh, my god. That's why you are so upset." He went over and gently held her face in his hands and made her look into his eyes. "I won't beat you. Do you understand? Never beat you."

She looked away.

He knelt down before her and held her hands in his. "I won't beat you. Hell, I won't sleep with you, if you don't want me to."

"Why you bring me hotel?"

"God, I just wanted to get you out of that place. You don't belong there. Here stretch out and go to sleep. I won't touch you."

She finally laid down on the bed and fell asleep

fully clothed with the bedspread pulled over her by Woody. He sat in the chair watching her for a long time before he fell asleep himself.

Woody was still in the chair when George knocked on the door in the morning. He stumbled to the door and let George in.

"Where in the hell did you go?" George said. "You missed a hell of a night," he laughed. "I tied up with some other guys, and we hit every bar on the street."

Woody looked around to see, if May Ling was decent. No one was in the bed, just the pulled-over bedspread and a dented pillow.

"May Ling? Where are you?"

George looked confused, as he watched Woody frantically search in the bathroom and around the room.

"Must have sneaked out while I was sleeping."

"What's going on?" George asked Woody.

"Damn girl. Slipped out on me."

"You paid for twenty-four hours?" George asked.

"That's not it." Woody whirled on George. "I wanted to take care of her. I wanted to protect her."

"Come on, Woody. She's a whore."

"No, she's not. She's just a kid."

"Come on. Let's go get some breakfast," George tried to lead Woody out of the room.

"I've got to find her. She can't go back to that joint. It'll ruin her."

"Come on. Let's discuss it over breakfast."

At breakfast George could not change Woody's mind. In fact, his arguments only made Woody firmer in his resolution to save May Ling. Woody finally decided to go to the club and buy May Ling. George told him that he was crazy.

"She isn't a dog or something," George said.

"I know. I know. But if I can buy her for a night,

why can't I buy her forever?"

"Why do you want her?"

"I just do."

"Give me one good reason."

"She smells good. No other woman smells right."

"Oh, my god. You're a goner. What did she do to you last night?"

"Nothing."

"Nothing?"

"Yes, nothing."

"You didn't do her?"

"No."

George was really puzzled now.

"I'm going to the Red Dragon and buy her."

"Christ. Think it over, Woody. Where are you going to put her?'

"I'll get her a nice place and send her to school where she belongs."

"You've lost your mind."

"Maybe I have," said Woody, as he left George to go buy May Ling for the price he had paid for a new convertible in the States. The owner of the bar was overjoyed, since he had only paid May Ling's father a small percentage of Woody's price when her father had dragged May Ling to his door a few months before. He had fattened her up and showed her how to dress and move, and look how it had worked out. She must have learned some good tricks with that old colonel who used whips and chains when he took her overnight. You have to beat them into submission. Just like dogs, he thought.

Woody and May Ling lived together for over six months. While he was flying missions, she studied at the Missionary School where the nuns never questioned Woody's relationship to her. He filled out the form and put himself down as her "protector." The sisters watched over her while he was gone, because he paid her tuition for a year ahead and gave a large donation to the church.

When Woody went stateside, he sent the nuns money, and letters and gifts to May Ling. She stopped writing to him four months ago, and the sisters reported that she had disappeared. His calls to the Red Dragon and the Bangkok police only proved to be expensive and frustrating. He never thought that he would see her again. The love of his life, he thought then.

Chapter B

Background Material

From "The Michigan Years," Hemingway in Michigan, Constance Cappel, Little Traverse Historical Society, Petoskey, MI. (third printing), pp. 3-10.

The Michigan Years

Ernest Hemingway first went to northern Michigan at the turn of the century, as a one-year-old taken by his parents to Walloon Lake. For many summers to come, the Hemingway family made the first leg of the journey to their summer home by lake steamer from Chicago to Harbor Springs, Michigan, on Little Traverse Bay.

Northern Michigan, a land of low,

rolling hills heavily forested with pines,
maples, and birches, dotted with clear lakes
and ponds, is bordered to the west by the
inland sea, which is Lake Michigan.
Lumbering camps, steamboats and working
schooners, horse-drawn farm wagons, a
pioneer life that Hemingway saw and
partially shared as a boy, no longer exist.
The land looks the same, and the wildness
of the storms over the lake and the
predominance of weather over the lives of
the people remains, but today superhighways
stretch upwards from Detroit towards the
sprawling bridge that crosses the Straits of
Mackinac. People from the cities seek their
rest in much greater numbers than in the
early 1900's, and the life of northern
Michigan is more gauged to them than to
the land. Hemingway loved this country.

Although many of the places in
Michigan, which Hemingway knew, have
changed, much of the countryside
described in his Michigan short stories and
in the one novel with a Michigan setting,
The Torrents of Spring, is exactly the same.
Although always an acute and accurate
reporter, in his early writings he became as
autobiographical as any writer of fiction can
be. Many of the people, as well as the places,
described in his writings existed and still
can be found. A farmhouse may have
burned down, but the farmer who owned it
will reminisce; a young Indian girl may be
dead for many years, but she remains in the
memory of others. From Hemingway's own

past and memories came his Michigan writings, and from these writings in turn the pattern of his early life is revealed. Northern Michigan is where he knew his first love, where he first seriously practiced writing, and where he lived when he returned from the First World War.

Harbor Springs, Michigan, in 1898 (approximately when the Hemingway's first came to the region) was emerging from a rough, pioneer lumber town into one of the most exclusive summer resorts in the United States. While the Eastern robber barons were building their castles of marble and stone in Newport, the wealthy industrialists of Detroit, Cincinnati, Lansing, St. Louis, and Chicago were building forty-room frame "cottages" on Harbor Point, a peninsula jutting into Little Traverse Bay.

Harbor Springs has probably changed less since Hemingway's infancy than any other town of the northern Michigan area he knew. The village grew quickly with the aid of the incoming wealth, and the same wealth, now in its fourth generation, has preserved the town as it was. In 1898 the lake steamers from Chicago would churn out of Lake Michigan into Little Traverse Bay, cross it, steam around Harbor Point, and drop anchor at Harbor Springs, the deepest natural harbor of the Great Lakes.

A spur of the Grand Rapids & Indiana Railroad connected the towns of Harbor Springs and Petoskey, eleven miles apart

around the bay. The Hemingway family
would carry their luggage from the dock to
the train for the ride to Petoskey. As Doctor
Hemingway and his family left the small,
frame railroad station in Harbor Springs
(which still stands), they probably enjoyed
the view of the placid harbor protected by
Harbor Point, with the clear and varicolored
blue water of Little Traverse Bay beyond.
The train would pass the dunes at the foot
of the bay and rumble through Bay View,
another resort. At Petoskey they again had
to transfer their luggage and change cars
for the train going to the village at Walloon
Lake, then Bear Lake.

The view from the train window would
be similar to the one now seen from the
window of an automobile. Far out on Lake
Michigan an ore carrier now leaves behind
a stream of smoke, as the large side-wheelers
once did. Closer into shore the waves still
beat on the rock shoals, and birch and pine
trees bend with the wind on shore. Petoskey,
the small town at the curve of the bay, still
stairsteps up the hills to the clear northern
sky.

Petoskey, the setting of Hemingway's
first published novel, *The Torrents of Spring*,
remains the small town he knew with many
of the same people living and working
there. The rooming house on State Street
where he lived and wrote in 1919 still stands.
The daughter of the original owner lived
in the house and liked to talk about her
family's famous guest, who was an unknown

writer when he lived there. Many other people living in Petoskey also liked to talk about the Ernest Hemingway they knew as a boy and a young man.

The highway out of Petoskey towards Charlevoix goes past a (formerly) dirt road. This road rises over the hills away from Little Traverse Bay to Walloon Lake and was described in the story "Ten Indians." Set deep in the trees on Walloon Lake is the Hemingway cottage where Ernest spent all of his summers from his first to his twenty-first year, except for the summer of 1918, when he was in Italy. One of his sisters used the cottage as her summer home.

With rolling hills surrounding it, Walloon Lake is considered one of the most beautiful of the smaller lakes in Michigan, but its character has changed since the days when Ernest Hemingway lived there. What was a rough outdoor setting for the Hemingway family is now a luxurious resort area where the "log cabins" sometimes run to twenty rooms. The lumber camp where the Indians worked and lived is gone as are the Indians who lived there. The steamers on Walloon Lake, which used to bring the Hemingways to their summer home, have disappeared.

Not far from Walloon Lake, on the road between Boyne City and Charlevoix, is the little town of Horton Bay which was the setting for the stories, "Up in Michigan," "The Three-Day Blow," and "The End of Something." The town was named for its

first settler, Samuel Horton. It has changed
little since the days when Hemingway
fished in Horton's Creek, lived at the
Dilworths' house, and eventually married
there. With its neat, frame houses painted
white, Horton Bay is the only locale in
Hemingway's Michigan which has remained
virtually untouched by tourists.

Ernest Hemingway was born on July 21,
1899. (He added a year to his age to obtain
a job on the Kansas City *Star*, so that his birth
date is often erroneously given as July 21,
1898.) With their young daughter and son,
Marcelline and Ernest, Doctor and Mrs.
Hemingway stayed at the Echo Beach Hotel
(which has since burned down) before they
built their summer cottage about a mile
down the shore of Bear Lake (now called
Walloon Lake).

Philip Young in his book about
Hemingway observed that "the parts of the
childhood which stuck were the
summertimes, which were spent in
Michigan." The "summertimes" and even
the other times of the year spent in
Michigan as the setting for ten published
stories, sections of two other stories, one
high school story (which only appeared
previously in an Oak Park High School
publication and is included in this book),
and a short novel.

Ernest's older sister, Marcelline,
remembered from what her parents told her
that they first went to Walloon Lake in August,
1898, when she was seven months old. The

Hemingways liked Walloon on their first visit
and bought four lots, equaling one acre.

Ernest's younger brother, Leicester,
who was sixteen years younger than Ernest
and also had gathered the information from
his parents, remembered it differently:

> *During the summer of 1900 our parents*
> *visited Walloon Lake in northern Michigan*
> *and were seized with a strange sense of shared*
> *destiny. They bought a tract of land; two*
> *acres of shore line more than four miles from*
> *the foot of the lake, which was then known as*
> *Bear Lake.*

According to Owen White, whose family
camped on the property next to the
Hemingways', the Hemingway cottage,
which was called "Windemere," was built by
1904, when Ernest was five. The Hemingway
cottage has changed superficially, but not
basically, since Ernest lived there. His sister,
Madeleine "Sunny" Hemingway Miller, who
still spent her summers there, explained:
"This place isn't anything like it was when
Ernie lived here. It was made of rough
timber and had a porch. I closed in the
breezeway. There wasn't any heat or
electricity back when we came up with our
father." She added, "Everything around
here has changed so much that Ernie
probably wouldn't be able to find his old
fishing spots over at Horton Bay."

When the cottage was built, according
to the late Marcelline Hemingway Sanford,

it included only a living room with a large
brick fireplace, a dining room, kitchen, two
bedrooms, and a roofed-over porch. The
exterior of the cottage was covered with
white clapboard and the interior with white
pine. A kitchen wing was added, and finally
the cottage had six bedrooms, three in an
annex.

Until 1917 Ernest lived an outdoor life
during the summers in Michigan. When
he was about sixteen he had his first love
affair, with an Indian girl in the Michigan
woods. During the summer of 1917, when
he became eighteen, Hemingway wanted
to enlist in the Army, but he had damaged
his eye when he was fourteen, while taking
boxing lessons in Chicago, and was rejected.
Instead of going to college in the autumn
of 1917, Ernest went to Kansas City and
worked as a reporter on the Kansas City *Star.*
He was a reporter there until the spring of
1918, when he decided to join the volunteer
ambulance unit of the Italian Army under
the auspices of the American Red Cross.
On April 30, he drew his last paycheck from
the *Star* and returned to northern Michigan
for a final fishing trip before going overseas.
Carl Edgar, a Horton Bay friend who had
worked for a fuel oil company in Kansas City
and had shared an apartment there with
Ernest during the winter of 1918, and
Charlie Hopkins, the Kansas City *Time's*
assignment editor, accompanied him.
Hemingway's orders were forwarded from
Kansas City to Horton Bay, and he left hastily

for New York City still wearing his fishing clothes.

On May 12 he was issued a uniform and was enlisted as an honorary lieutenant in the Italian Army. In late May of 1918 he sailed for Europe. Serving on the Italian front as an ambulance driver, he went through some of the bitterest fighting of the War. Badly wounded at Fossalta di Piave, Ernest was hospitalized at Milan and decorated by the Italians with their most coveted medal, the *Medaglia d'Argento al Valore Militare*, equivalent to the French *Medaille Militaire*, and with three *Croci al Merito di Guerra*.

After the War, Hemingway returned to the United States on January 21, 1919, to recuperate. Since he had been injured at night, Ernest was not able to sleep in the dark for a long time. He went to Michigan in March of that year and then lived with his family off and on during the following summer. At this time he became emotionally involved with a girl from Petoskey who was fictionalized in several of his stories. In the fall he remained in Horton Bay at the Dilworth's' house and picked potatoes for a living. He moved to Petoskey during the winter of 1919-1920 where he lived at Potter's Rooming House at 602 State Street. Hazel Potter, who was working in nearby Mancelona that winter, remembers that when she was home visiting on weekends, she often heard Hemingway "typing away all the time in his front corner room."

"I put in a fall and half a winter writing up in Petoskey, Michigan," Hemingway said many years later, describing the extent of the preparation which preceded his first expatriate publication in 1923. It was a period of discouraging rejection. "I worked and wrote," he said on another occasion, "and couldn't sell anything."

During this winter, Hemingway concentrated on his writing, but he also visited and had dinner with many Petoskey friends. At the Pailthorps, Hemingway met Ralph Connable, a personable American who headed Woolworth of Canada. In an interview with Frances Pailthorp, William Forrest Dawson wrote, "Connable asked about taking 'Dutch' Pailthorp back to Toronto with him. Dutch couldn't go himself, so he suggested his pal, Ernest." Hemingway did not want to go back to his family in Chicago, so that about halfway through the winter he went to Toronto as a tutor for Connable's young son. Hemingway lived with the Connables in Toronto, and through Ralph Connable got his job with the Toronto *Star,* which subsequently took him back to Europe.

Returning to Michigan for the summer and early autumn of 1920, Ernest gathered material for the fishing and camping series which was published in the Toronto *Star Weekly*. His twenty-first birthday, which proved to be an eventful one, occurred during that summer.

In the fall of 1920, Hemingway went back to Chicago, where he lived in an apartment on the North Side, and it was there that he met Sherwood Anderson. He obtained a job editing the house organ of the Co-operative Society of America. While he lived in Chicago, he met Hadley Richardson, who was to become his first wife.

In September of 1921, Hemingway returned to Michigan for his last long visit. (Hemingway made only brief trips to Michigan after 1921.) On September 3, 1921, he married Hadley Richardson. After a two-week honeymoon at the Hemingway cottage on Walloon Lake, the couple moved to Chicago, then to Toronto, and finally to Paris.

Many of the more important events of Hemingway's formative years occurred in Michigan, where he learned to fish, hunt, drink, know girls, and even to concentrate seriously on his writing. Hemingway, like one of the migratory birds which he hunted, always returned to Michigan in the summer. When he returned to the United States after being wounded in the First World War, he withdrew himself like a hurt animal and healed his wounds in the solitude of a boarding house in Petoskey. When he took his therapeutic fishing trips, he fished in northern Michigan streams. Finally, when he found the woman to be his wife, he married her in Horton Bay, Michigan. The pattern is one of almost compulsive return to the home of the growing writer, Ernest Hemingway.

*   *   *

From *History of the Ottawa and Chippewa Indians of Michigan, Little Traverse Historical Society,* Petoskey, MI.

However it was a notable fact that by this time the Ottawas were greatly reduced in numbers from what they were in former times, on account of the smallpox which they brought from Montreal during the French war with Great Britain. This small pox was sold to them shut up in a tin box, with the strict injunction not to open the box on their way homeward, but only when they should reach their country; and that this box contained something that would do them great good, and their people! The foolish people believed really there was something in the box supernatural, that would do them great good. Accordingly, after they reached home, they opened the box; but behold there was another tin box inside, smaller. They took it out and opened the second box, and behold, still there was another box inside of the second box, smaller yet. So they kept on this way till they came to a very small box, which was not more than an inch long; and when they opened the last one they found nothing but muddy particles in this last little box! They wondered very much what it was, and a great many closely inspected to try to find out what it meant. But alas, alas! Pretty soon burst out

a terrible sickness among them. The great
Indian doctors themselves were taken sick
and died. The tradition says it was indeed
awful and terrible. Every one taken with it
was sure to die. Lodge after lodge was totally
vacated—nothing but the dead bodies lying
here and there in their lodges-entire
families being swept off with the ravages of
this terrible disease. The whole coast of
Arbor Croche, or Waw-gaw-naw-ke-zee,
where their principal village was situated,
on the west shore of the peninsula near the
Straits, which is said to have been a
continuous village some fifteen or sixteen
miles long and extending from what is now
called Cross Village to Seven-Mile Point
(that is, seven miles from Little Traverse,
now Harbor Springs), was entirely
depopulated and laid waste. It is generally
believed among the Indians of Arbor
Croche that this wholesale murder of the
Ottawas by this terrible disease sent by the
British people, was actuated through
hatred, and expressly to kill off the Ottawas
and Chippewas because they were friends
of the French Government or French King,
whom they called "Their Great Father." The
reason that today we see no full-grown trees
standing along the coast of Arbor Croche, a
mile or more in width along the shore, is
because the trees were entirely cleared away
for this famous long village, which existed
before the small pox raged among the
Ottawas.

Chapter III

THE MITCHELLS

Trudy ducked between the cedar trees and took the footpath through the woods to Indian town. Her house was only two blocks from the Little Harbor Club, but it was a world away.

She ran through her uncut yard filled with broken toys and two abandoned cars before she climbed up the broken wooden steps to the two-story house covered with tarpaper. Dick Mitchell always promised to cut the grass, haul away the autos, put siding on the house, get a regular job, quit drinking, and change his habits. He did cut the grass once.

Trudy's mother, Irene Tabeshaw, who called herself Mrs. Mitchell, was in the kitchen when Trudy came through the torn screen door. She just looked at Trudy and passed her the baby on her hip.

Trudy held the crying child away from her, because his diapers were soiled. She took him into the bathroom and put him in the tub to clean him off. She didn't blame her mother, but it was increasingly hard to come home. She wished that she could just live in her wild rose bower on the side of the hill and be by herself and read all the time.

But now that she had the baby clean, she knew that she had to help her mother cook dinner. When she came back into the kitchen, her mother sank into a chair and began nursing the baby. Trudy looked into the refrigerator. Not much. Then she pulled open the storage drawer at the bottom of the refrigerator and pulled out enough potatoes to fill half a large pot. She walked outside and pulled up some dandelion greens, and she had enough for dinner. Soon the garden she had planted would be helping her put healthy food on the table.

Trudy looked at her mother who looked older than her years. She was fat, and her hair that she pulled back from her round face with the high cheekbones was gray. Her uncles told Trudy that her mother was "quite a looker until Dick Mitchell got a hold of her."

"Mom. How are you feeling?"

"Tired."

"Go in and listen to the radio."

"No."

"Why not?"

"Too tired."

"Mom, you have to do something for yourself sometime."

"No time."

Trudy just looked away.

"Mom. Did you take your medicine?"

"No."

"Why?"

"Ran out. Too expensive."

Trudy couldn't argue with her, but knew she had to take the blood pressure medicine.

"Did Dad come back?"

"No."

Dick Mitchell had been gone for two days. He came and went as he chose.

"Just as well," Trudy said.

"Did you talk to Sister Elizabeth?" Her mother asked.

"No."

"Why not?"

"Too busy."

"Busy doing nothing. You need a job. We need money."

Sister Elizabeth had told her mother at Mass that she had work for Trudy helping with the younger children at the Mission School. Trudy worked every summer as a babysitter on the Point, but this summer she just did not want to take care of her brothers and sisters and some rich families' children too. She was tired of taking care of kids. She wanted to use her mind.

"Sister Elizabeth wants you to come to Mass."

"I know."

"What makes you so difficult?"

"I'm not difficult. Just different."

"Better than your mother."

"No, not better than you."

"Too much Alice Mitchell."

"Aunt Alice is nice."

"Not a Catholic."

"No. Not a Catholic."

"I'm finished." Her mother put the baby on the couch to sleep and called the others to dinner.

After Trudy fed everyone, cleaned up, and did the dishes, she still had time to do some weeding in the garden before the late sunset.

She decided to walk into town on this Saturday night and look at the boats in the Harbor. She liked sitting in Zorn Park and looking out at the Point at dusk. Beyond the big boat sheds she could see the lights come on and reflect in the water. Around ten o'clock she could hear the music from the band at the Little Harbor Club float over the water. She would become invisible in the neat mowed grass of Zorn Park and lose herself in the twinkling lights on the water and in the ones in the clear northern Michigan sky. The cool air off the water and the crisp chill of night made her wrap her arms around herself and wonder what she was going to do now.

Trudy had always made plans, and now she had no plan. She had always worked hard in school, so that she could go to college. Now she was out of high school and had not even applied to any college. She had always had a summer job, but now she did not want to baby-sit. She felt exhausted with her mother. When she brought her money home, Irene sometimes gave it to her father. He would then go drinking, and no one would benefit. Dick Mitchell took odd jobs painting and doing carpentry, but the summer people quit hiring him when he never finished a job. He was always in the Pier Bar bragging and drinking and playing pool. Trudy used to go down to get him when she was a child. Now she did not care, if he came home. He would just fight with her mother and get her pregnant again.

Trudy had decided never to get married or have children. She was a virgin, not by accident. When she was younger, she was a tomboy and could out

wrestle and beat up any boy her age in Harbor. But
then they started growing, and she stayed the same
height. Several of the boys that she had beaten up
when she was younger sought her out and
demolished her when Trudy grew older. But Trudy
had learned enough to defend herself, and what the
other girls saw as "love," she saw as hand-to-hand
combat. All of her wrestling skills she applied to
wriggling out from under drunken football players
and twisting and jabbing in the backseat of cars. Not
that she did not like to kiss and make out, but when
the boys went to "second base," she got loose. No
one ever came close to "third base." Despite that she
was known as "hot" and a good date. She always had
two or three boys ask her to parties and the prom,
but she never "went steady" and did not think much
of the girls who did. If you went steady, she thought,
you slept with the boy, hung his class ring on a chain
around your neck, and had a better chance of being
chosen as the prom queen.

Trudy was never a prom queen, but always a
member of the prom court. She was never a
cheerleader, but attended all of the football and
basketball games. She always had boy friends, but
never "a boyfriend." The girls liked her, but she never
was in the inner circle. Trudy Mitchell was a loner
and lived in her own world. Her world was in the
books she read.

From the books she had ideas that no one knew
about and she never shared. No one knew that Trudy
was just waiting for a chance to escape Harbor
Springs. She thought that she would go to the
University of Michigan and then get a job in New
York City. She liked the way Fitzgerald described New
York in *The Great Gatsby* and the short story "The Rich

Boy." She wanted to go to the Plaza Hotel, the Stork Club, El Morocco, and go to Sardis after the theater. She read the expensive magazines that the summer people left out, and she went to the movies at the Lyric Theater on Main Street.

Her aunt Alice always told her that she was a dreamer and that she should set realistic sights. Her aunt Alice was delighted that Trudy was not going to waste her time going to college. Lately she had been hinting to Trudy to think more seriously about Johnnie Moore who had taken her to the senior prom. His father owned the five and dime store, and Johnnie was going to take it over some day. Right now he was working there until college started in the autumn.

When Trudy told her that she did not love Johnnie Moore, Alice Mitchell said: "Marry first. Love will come later. Besides it is better to marry someone who loves you more than you love them. Gives you the upper hand."

This philosophy of marrying young to someone who loved her more had proved to be a good choice for Alice Mitchell. She had married Ben Mitchell, right out of high school, and they were married for almost thirty-five years. Ben Mitchell adored Alice and still called her his "little chickadee." Trudy sometimes watched them and wondered what it would be like to wake up every morning for almost thirty-five years to see Ben Mitchell's hangdog face on the pillow next to you. Not that Ben Mitchell was not nice, but Trudy could not stand all of the billing and cooing that went on between them. They never had any children, so that they doted on each other and a succession of cats.

Trudy rolled on her stomach and touched the

dew on the grass. She did not want to go home, but it was getting cold down near the black water. She decided to walk over to the Pier Bar and see whether her father was there. Trudy had practically grown up in the bar, since Dick Mitchell had used her as a cover when she was young. He would tell Irene that they were going to see "Snow White" or "Dumbo" at the Lyric and then leave halfway through for the bar. Trudy had to read the books to see what happened in the second half of all those Walt Disney films.

But Trudy liked the Pier Bar, since she could have all of the free Cokes she could drink. Butch Callahan owned the bar and had a daughter Trudy's age. He also took care of his little girl on Saturdays when Dick and Trudy would come down. Patsy Callahan had dimples and curls like Shirley Temple, and her father would put her up on the bar where she would sing the "Good Ship Lollipop." Sometimes Trudy was placed on the bar, but since she looked more like a quieter Margaret O'Brien, she would just watch Patsy tap dance and show off.

Patsy Callahan was "knocked up" in her junior year by one of the Flanagan boys and the last time that Trudy saw her she was walking a baby carriage. Trudy felt sorry for her. She knew that Patsy would not be at the Pier Bar tonight.

When she walked in, all of the regulars were there, and, yes, Dick Mitchell was among them. He looked medium drunk, so that she walked over to him.

"Your mother sent you?"

"No."

"What are you doing here then?"

"Just felt like it."

"How about a Coke, Trudy?" Don Miller, who was

two years ahead of her in high school, and now was a bartender, asked her.

"Sure, why not? A Coke, please."

Dick Mitchell was a good-looking man even at his age. His hair was straight and black without gray, and he had a tall, rangy body. Trudy had inherited her father's lanky, graceful body with the long arms and legs. She had none of her mother's short, pudgy frame, but she did have the round Tabeshaw face, high cheekbones, and bronze skin. The men in the bar considered Trudy a beauty.

"Dick Mitchell how could such an ugly cuss like you have a daughter like this?" said Al Johnson, as he patted on a bar stool for Trudy to sit down next to him.

"Just lucky, I guess."

"Did you see 'Fay's Folly' almost hit the Coast Guard cutter when it was coming in?"

"Nope."

"Crazy Florida crew doesn't know anything. They should hire up here and take us down like they used to do."

"The Cubans are probably cheaper."

"Nobody could be cheaper than us."

"Spics are."

Dick Mitchell always wanted to go to Florida for the winter. Mr. Fay knew of his reputation and never hired him.

"So Trudy, what are you up to?" asked Al Johnson.

"Not much."

"Babysitting this summer?"

"No, I'm sick of kids."

"Don't blame you," he laughed.

"Going to college in the fall?"

"No."

"Why not? You're a smart girl."

"I don't know."

"Money?"

"Uh-huh."

"That's why I started at the garage after high school and never left. Twenty years now."

"How can you stand it, Al?"

"What do you mean?" He looked at her, surprised at her question.

"The same job for twenty years, the same town. The same guys at the bar. Everything."

"I dunno. Seems kinda nice to me. I like fixing cars. I like Harbor, and I like the guys. It's home."

"Well, Al, it isn't enough for me. I want more."

Al was getting uneasy with her intensity. "Let's play pool, Trudy."

They went over to the billiard table in the other room facing out on the water. Trudy moved deftly around the table and held her own.

When she and Al went back to the bar, they noticed that a bunch of summer people had come in. Usually the summer residents stayed to themselves and sat at the round table in the corner. They always drank bourbon or some kind of whiskey and water while the women drank gin tonics and rum and cokes. They usually played all the latest hits on the Wurlitzer, and always played "Sleeptime Girl" which was written right up the street at Juilleret's in the roaring Twenties. "Sleeptime Girl" was playing when Trudy and Al Johnson reentered the noisy bar. The smell of spilt beer and heavy cigarette smoke filled the now crowded bar.

Trudy slithered through the crowd on her way back to the bar. The bar crowd was two deep, so that she and Al joined a group at a table. Mostly men from the garage and their wives, Trudy fit in despite their twenty-year age difference. She had always seemed older than her years and now that she was full grown, she could have been in her twenties as well as seventeen. Even the liquor inspector did not realize her age. One night he sat next to her at the bar and complained about all of the teenagers with their fake I.D.s.

She dropped down next to Jill Turner, Bob Turner's wife.

"How's it going, Trudy?"

"Not bad."

"Hear from any those colleges?"

"Didn't apply."

"Why you were all fired up about going down state to college."

"Changed my mind."

"Smart. Why don't you go to hairdressing school and join me in the shop?"

"Thanks. That's an idea."

"Believe me, it works. I worked through two pregnancies, and since it is my shop, no man could send me home."

"Uh-huh." Trudy looked absent-mindedly over the Saturday night crowd. The place was jammed on this cool evening in northern Michigan on the shortest night of the year.

"Hear you are seeing Johnnie Moore?"

"Uh-huh."

"Nice boy. Good marriage material."

"Uh-huh."

"Working down at his father's store."

"Uh-huh."

"You and he make a nice pair."

"I don't think so."

"What do you mean? He is a nice, clean boy from a good Christian family."

"I know."

"You could do a lot worse."

Trudy thought, "And a lot better." She liked Johnnie, but when he kissed her and his Old Spice clung to her clothes, she could not wait to get away. Not that he was not pleasant company, but when he kept recounting the inventory of the store over and over, she just wanted to yell. She knew that everyone expected her to marry Johnnie and that some day she would regret it, but she knew something better was waiting for her. But then again maybe she was just a dreamer like her Aunt Alice said.

At that moment Woody and the group of people from the Little Harbor Club he was leading, entered the Pier Bar. He looked around the room, checking the crowd, seeing where the potential trouble stood. He guided his flock to the safe table in the corner to join the other summer residents, and then went up to the bar for drinks. Trudy watched him.

She liked to watch people when they did not know they were being watched. That was when you found out what they were really like. They weren't acting then or trying to impress you.

Trudy watched Woody cross the crowded room in front of her. She liked the way he moved, invisible and prowling, among the crowd. She liked the way he unobtrusively edged his way close to the bar. She liked the way he protected himself with his elbow on the bar while he had his back to the mirrored wall at the end of the bar. She liked the way he surveyed the crowd with his cool wolf eyes. He was as quiet as Dick Mitchell was loud at the other end of the bar.

Suddenly she was on her feet. Trudy could now

see her reflection in the mirrored glass. She could
see Dick Mitchell at one end of the bar, and she could
see Woody at the other. Both men saw her. She felt
drawn into some fateful triangle not of her own
making. The two men warily watched her approach
the center of the bar, both watching for tell tale signs
of drunkenness. Trudy walked straight and sure-
footed. Both looked ahead to her target, who she
was moving towards at the bar. Dick Mitchell did not
see any problems among his friends at the bar. Woody
straightened up, as he saw her approach the
unkempt group of locals. He was poised.

Trudy threw herself into the midst of flannel-
shirted men. She kidded them and watched Woody
watching her from the end of the bar. She got
another Coke and watched him staring at her. She
stared back. Trudy then looked down at her drink
and then slowly looked up again. She smiled shyly at
him.

Woody left all of the drinks he had ordered for
his table and told the waiter to take them over to his
friends. He worked his way around to Trudy's side.

"Hello again," he said to her.

She was shy and looked down at her feet.

"Quite a crowd tonight," he offered.

"Uh-huh."

"You come here often?"

"Uh-huh."

"Any of these guys your guy?"

"No."

"My name's Woody. What's yours?"

"Trudy. I told you before."

"That's an unusual name."

"Prudence."

"That's even more unusual."

"Uh-huh."

"Where did you get a name like that?"

"My aunt."

"Is that your aunt's name?"

"Yes. Prudence Mitchell."

"She live here?"

"No. She's dead. Lived near Charlevoix."

"I'm sorry."

"It is okay. She's been dead a long time."

"What of?"

"Some say broken heart. Some say she killed herself."

"What do you think?"

"Don't know."

At that moment Bitsy Fay came up to Woody and dragged him back to their table.

"See you, Trudy," he said, as Bitsy threaded him away across the floor.

Dick Mitchell glowered at the Pointer who had talked to his daughter and asked Jimmy Gaylord who Woody was. Jimmy was one of the caretakers on the Point and knew everyone.

"That's Woody Woodward. A real wild man. Rich, too."

"They all are," Dick grumbled.

"No, he's *real* rich."

"Wild?"

"Yes. Been everywhere. Done everything."

"I'll keep my eye on him," Dick said. "Trudy's only seventeen.

Chapter C

From "The Bacons and Prudence," *Hemingway in Michigan*, pp. 84-93.

Two of Hemingway's Michigan stories are based on his relationships with some of his Walloon Lake neighbors: the Bacons, a farming family, and Prudence, the Indian girl of the Indian camp. In the story "Fathers and Sons," a mature Nicholas Adams remembers his first sexual relationship, which had been with the Indian girl. In "Ten Indians" young Nick Adams is riding in the Garners' farm wagon, and he later learns that Prudence has been unfaithful to him.

The story "Ten Indians" was first published in *Men Without Women* a collection of short stories published by Scribner's on October 14, 1927. Hemingway in an interview once said:

I wrote "Ten Indians" after writing "The Killers" in Madrid on May 16 when it snowed out the San Isidro bullfights. . . . I had so much juice I thought maybe I was going crazy and I had about six other stories to write. So I got dressed and walked to Fornos, the old bull fighter's cafe, and drank coffee and then came back and wrote "Ten Indians." This made me very sad and I drank some brandy and went to sleep.

Why did this story make him very sad? Probably for two reasons: One was the remembrance of his unhappy home situation, and the other was that it made him remember how he felt after his first girl friend had been unfaithful to him.

The "Joe Garner" in "Ten Indians" resembles Joe Bacon in real life, and everything in this story points to the fact that Joe Garner is modeled after Joe Bacon. Joseph Bacon's father built a log cabin and began his farm on Walloon Lake in 1878. Joe Bacon said that he sold some lakefront property to Doctor Hemingway in 1895, which differs from both Marcelline's date of 1898 and Leicester's of 1900.

Mrs. George Depew, the former Myrtle Dale, lived in 1960 on Depew Road, which is about a mile behind the Hemingway cottage. A lifelong resident of the area, she knew both the Bacon family and Prudence. Mrs. Depew remembered: "The Bacon barn burnt down about twenty-five years ago, and the house was torn down afterwards. The

Bacons settled there in 1880. The first resort cottage on Walloon Lake was built in 1878. The Bacon farmhouse was frame and painted white while the barn was painted red. The Bacon property ran down to the lake right next to the Hemingway land."

John McConnell also remembered the Bacon family: "'Doc' Hemingway drove the last spike at Bacon's barnraising and was proud of that and talked about it a lot. Everyone said, 'the Bacons feed the Hemingways, but they get their doctoring for free!' Doctor Hemingway kept a garden over at their place on the other side of the lake that they called 'Longfield,' because of its long field. One summer Ernie rowed around to the cottages on the lake and came up to the hotel with a load of vegetables he was trying to sell. So the Bacons didn't supply the Hemingways with all their food. Joe Bacon always judges the chickens at the Emmet County Fair and says, 'I've never missed a fair.' He must be about ninety now."

In "Ten Indians" Nick is driving home from Petoskey in the Garners' big wagon. As they drive along, they pass nine drunken Indians on the road. (The tenth Indian of the title is Nick's girl, Prudence.) Joe Garner pulls the horses to a halt and drags one Indian out of the wheel rut, where he had fallen asleep with his face in the sand.

Joe Bacon remembered one night when he and his family were returning home in what he also called the "big wagon," and they passed a squaw who was "dead drunk and lying face down in the middle of the road." Mrs. Bacon said, according to her husband, "Just run her over, she ain't worth nothing no how." Joe Bacon stopped the wagon and lifted the Indian woman to the side of the road. The next morning, when he asked the squaw about it, she did not remember anything of the night before.

Billy Tabeshaw, who appeared before in "The Doctor and the Doctor's Wife" and "Sepi Jingan," is again mentioned in this story. Carl Garner wonders whether one of the drunken Indians was Bill Tabeshaw, but either Nick Adams or Frank Garner (the speaker is not identified) says that it is not Billy. But Carl thinks that the Indian's pants looked like Billy's, and the unidentified speaker (probably Nick) then makes the pronouncement that Indians all wear the same type of pants.

The route of the farm wagon going from Petoskey to Resort Pike Road in "Ten Indians" can be followed today by the same landmarks described in the story. As they drive along in the wagon, the road turns off the main highway and leads up into the hills. At this point the horses have to pull hard, and the boys have to get out and walk on the sandy road. Then Nick looks back from the hilltop by the schoolhouse and sees the lights of Petoskey and, off across Little Traverse Bay, the lights of Harbor Springs. (Hemingway sometimes spelled "Harbour Springs" with the British "u," but all records and maps indicate that it has always been spelled "Harbor Springs.") In the story the boys climb back into the wagon, and Joe Garner suggests that gravel should be put on that part of the road, probably to insure better traction.

Joseph Bacon was able to pinpoint the entire trip, since three roads offer a route past a schoolhouse and a night view of both Harbor Springs and Petoskey. "When we came from Petoskey in the horse and wagon," Bacon said, "we would come up Washout Road then cross over to Resort Pike where the Greig schoolhouse is on the corner." The original landmarks on this most direct and logical of the three possible routes are exactly as they were described by Hemingway in "Ten Indians." The young Hemingway had traveled with Joseph Bacon is his wagon over the exact route which Joe Garner and Nick Adams follow in the story.

Earlier in the story Hemingway mentioned the two Garner boys, "Carl" and "Frank." Joseph Bacon had six children, one boy named Earl and another named Carl, but he did not have a son named Frank. Carl Garner, who teases the young Nick Adams about his Indian girl, is the principal speaker of the two Garner boys. In real life, Carl Bacon was Hemingway's friend. The experience which formed the inspiration for this story probably happened when Hemingway was about sixteen or seventeen. Joseph Bacon recalled that "Ernie and Carl were always playing together and making a mess out in the wheat shucks when they were young."

But when the action in this story took place, Nick Adams and Carl Garner were not interested in playing in the wheat shucks. They had a more interesting topic of conversation, girls. In this story the girl discussed is the Indian girl "Prudence Mitchell."

Mrs. George Depew taught school in the one-room schoolhouse of Resort District in 1911, when Hemingway was twelve. At this little schoolhouse, which has since been torn down, Mrs. Depew had in her classes a little Indian girl, Prudence Bolton, who was about ten years old, which meant she was two years younger than Hemingway. Prudence Bolton, according to the people who knew her, was Dick Bolton's daughter which would make her one-fourth French and three-fourths Indian. As a child of ten, Prudence was supposed to have had nice skin, long, black hair, and to be pretty.

Another Indian family at the camp was the Mitchells, but they did not have a Prudence Mitchell among them. The Mitchells were related to the Boltons, since Dan Mitchell's wife was a Tabeshaw and so was Dick Bolton's wife. When Hemingway named Nick's Indian girlfriend, he probably changed Prudence Bolton's last name to Mitchell. Since there were no other girls named "Prudence" living in the Indian camp, Prudence Bolton "Mitchell." Years later Hemingway gave his wife, Mary, a compliment, by telling her that she had legs "just like Trudy Bolton's."

While Nick, Carl, and Mr. And Mrs. Garner converse, Hemingway describes their progress in the wagon along Resort Pike. At one point when the horses pull hard in the sand, Joe Garner whips them. This is on a steep incline where the horses would have had to pull heavily. Later on in the story the horses trot down a long hill with the wagon jolting. Resort Pike follows the same route today.

In the story Mr. And Mrs. Garner are a happily married couple who tease each other. Their warm relationship is also shown in their attitude toward their children and the neighbor boy, Nick. Their home is a happy home, in contrast to the one of Nick Adams as described in "The Doctor and the Doctor's Wife." When Nick leaves the Garners' farmhouse to go to his own house, Mrs. Garner asks him to send Carl, who is outside unloading the wagon, to the house. When Nick goes down to the barn to thank Joe Garner for the good time he had, Nick casually tells him to tell Carl his mother wants him. It is assumed that Carl will be given this message and go to his mother. The naturalness of this request of the mother and response of the son is in direct contrast to the reactions of Nick to the same request at the end of "The Doctor and the Doctor's Wife."

In "Ten Indians" Nick takes the familiar walk from the Garners' farmhouse to his

parents' summer cottage: through the
meadow which is below the Garners' barn,
over a fence at the end of the meadow, then
down through a ravine where he gets his
feet wet in the swamp mud. Then he climbs
up through the beech woods (which still
surround the Hemingway cottage), until he
sees the lights of the cottage. (This route is
the same one Nick Adams traveled in the
story, "Fathers and Sons.") Nick's father is
by himself, reading in the kitchen, when
Nick comes in and brings Nick his dinner
of cold chicken, milk, and huckleberry pie.
His mother does not appear in this story.

As Nick and his father sit in the kitchen
talking, Nick asks his father what he had
done during the day. The father answers
that he went for a walk near the Indian
camp; when Nick quizzes him as to whether
he had seen anyone, Doctor Adams notes
noncommittally that all of the Indians were
in town getting drunk. When Nick presses
him, he answers that he had seen Nick's
friend Prudie "threshing around" in the
woods with a boy named Frank Washburn.

Nick begins crying when his father
leaves the room. Adams sees his son in tears,
he tries to comfort him by offering him some
more pie and then suggesting that Nick go
to bed. In his room Nick feels that his heart
is broken, but he feels well enough to
observe that a cool wind has come up. After
a while he forgets to think about Prudence
and falls asleep. In the middle of the night
Nick awakes to hear the wind in the trees,

but goes back to sleep. By morning a strong wind is blowing, and the waves are coming far up the beach, and he is awake for a long time before he remembers his grief.

A poem, "Along With Youth," which Hemingway wrote in Paris and which appeared in *Three Stories and Ten Poems,* captures the same sentiments about lost youth and young love that are aroused in "Ten Indians." Most of the images in the poem come from northern Michigan, and some are the same as in the story.

In "Fathers and Sons" Hemingway described a route that he had often taken from the family cottage on Walloon Lake to the hemlock woods behind the Indian camp. Nick Adams follows the same route to the trysting place with the Indian girl. The route can be followed on foot today, although the fences and the Bacons' barn have disappeared. The pine-needle loam is still underfoot in the hemlock woods behind the Hemingway cottage and fallen logs still crumble into wood dust. Pieces of splintered wood still hang like javelins from a large, lightning-struck tree, probably not the same one the young boy passed, but one which brings to mind the tree in the story. The small creek runs nearby, crossed by a log. If you were to slip from the log, you would still step into the black swamp muck.

Proceeding northwest to the left, you would still find the swampy creek bottom. The fence that the young Hemingway climbed over has disappeared, but you still come out of the woods and on to the place where the field for grazing used to be. The field is now overgrown and full of wildflowers. You go by the barn, over another fence, past the house, and down the sandy road which went into the woods. The sandy road, which is still hot underfoot in summer, runs from the site of the former farmhouse to the woods, but now it runs past rows of planted Christmas trees.

The Bacon farmhouse no longer stands on the site, but Joseph Bacon had an oil painting of it. In his small house in Petoskey in 1960, he dug through a pile of assorted souvenirs of his past, which were stacked in a corner of his living room, and came out with a painting of his homestead. When asked, not volunteering the information himself, who had done the painting, Bacon answered, "Mrs. Hemingway." Without knowing it, Ernest Hemingway's mother had painted in oils the exact landscape which her son had meticulously described in both "Ten Indians" and "Fathers and Sons."

But Nick's trip in "Fathers and Sons" is not over. After he passes the Garners' farm, he continues towards his teenage Indian girlfriend. He goes into the woods on the clay and shale road, off the main road, which turns to the left, and goes around the woods and then climbs the hill. The actual road to the Indian camp was broad at the point where the Indians slide out the hemlock bark they cut.

Hemingway, with his facility for total recall and accurate description, has caught in "Fathers and Sons," in eighty-four words the color, smell, physical appearance, and purpose of the Indian lumber camp. Other neighbors and members of the Hemingway family have all described the Indian camp, but only Ernest was able to capture it as it was, even predicting its demise within his eighty four words. The hemlock forest around the camp has long since been destroyed by the Indian barkpeelers, who took the bark to the tannery in Boyne City, as the Indians did in Hemingway's story. The buildings of the camp and all of the Indians have also disappeared. And now nothing remains in the maple woods except grown-over roads and man-moved earth—roads leading nowhere and useless earth barricades.

The next section of the story is a description of what Theodore Bardacke writes is "the one satisfying sexual relationship of the volume *(Winner Take Nothing).* This is an adolescent union with a little Indian girl who is submissive and devoid of any real individual personality." The Indian girl in this story is called "Trudy," which is very close to the "Prudence" and "Prudie" of "Ten Indians." She has a brother named Billy Gilby, who shoots with Nick's gun while Nick makes love to his sister. The two Indians mention an older half-breed brother named Eddie Gilby, who is seventeen. Trudy's age is

established as having been about fifteen at
the time of the incident Nick remembers
in "Fathers and Sons." This would
correspond to the age of Prudence Bolton
at the time she and Hemingway were seen
together. There was a Billy Mitchell, an
Indian who lived at the lumber camp, and
the name of the previously mentioned
Indian family of Gilberts is similar to Gilby.
Prudence Bolton also had a brother Eddy,
who was a half-breed, as she was.

Nick makes love to Trudy on a
hemlock-needled bed in the woods while
Billy, her brother, lies near them.
Afterwards, Nick is happy, until Trudy
tells him that her older half-brother wants
to sleep with his (Nick's) sister. It is all
right if Nick has an affair with Trudy, but
this is another thing. Equality is over. Nick
is furious. He threatens to kill Eddie
Gilby, whom he calls a "half-breed
bastard." Trudy becomes upset and
pleads with Nick not to kill her half-
brother, but Nick is enjoying his role and
enacts the whole, imaginary murder, even
to the point of scalping Eddie Gilby. Billy
notes that Nick is just a big bluff, and Nick
finally agrees with Trudy that he would
not murder Eddie unless he came near
the Adams house.

Trudy is relieved and wants to make love
again. This time Nick sends Billy away with
the gun. After they make love, Trudy
wonders whether they had made a baby.
When Nick answers negatively, she says in

slang that it does not make any difference if she becomes pregnant.

Mrs. Depew, who had taught the ten-year-old Prudence Boulton in the one-room schoolhouse of the Resort District, remembered distinctly what eventually happened to Prudence: "Prudence never married, but died when she was young. I don't know how, since I was away from home at the time. When I asked them about her, my parents told me that she had died. She never finished high school. Prudence was a pretty girl, but many Indian girls are more attractive when they are young. She had nice skin, long, black hair, and looked like a full-blooded Indian."

Some of the people who knew Prudence said that she died in childbirth, and one even said that the rumor had gone around that it was Ernest Hemingway's child Prudence was carrying. She was buried in Bay Shore, according to her neighbors, and a "priest prayed over her grave."

Nick's little boy in "Fathers and Sons" asks his father about how it was when he used to hunt with the Indians. Nick tells him that his father only gave him three shells, so that he would learn to hunt. Nick adds that he used to go out nearly every day hunting black squirrels with Billy Gilby and Trudy. When his son questions him further about the Indians, Nicholas Adams is unable to tell his son about his sexual experience with Trudy.

When Hemingway wrote about Trudy

and his memories of her, he wrote in abbreviated "Indian talk." Later in his life Hemingway often lapsed into Indian talk, which caused some critics, notably Lillian Ross in her *New Yorker* interview, to ridicule him for what they seemed to consider an affectation. Since the young writer had spent many of his formative years among the Ojibwas and had spoken their language, his Indian talk was not an affectation, but an integral part of his own speech and writing patterns.

Nick felt that jokes about Indian girls, old squaws, and the sick-sweet smell they get could not take away what he once felt for Trudy. Hemingway wrote in "Fathers and Sons" about what happened to Indian girls. "Not what they did finally. It wasn't how they ended. They all ended the same. Long time ago good. Now no good."

Although "what they did finally" could be construed as the actions of Prudence in "Ten Indians," it seems doubtful that Hemingway knew what finally became of Prudence Bolton. Becoming promiscuous and a fat squaw is apparently what became of many pretty, young Indian girls in northern Michigan, but from the testimony of the neighbors, this was not Prudence's fate.

The wooden crosses over the remaining Indian graves in the lonely, roadside town of Bay Shore are unmarked. Now Bay Shore is just a few houses in the middle of wild, overgrown fields on the highway from Petoskey to Charlevoix, and none of the people there knew about Prudence Bolton. Indian deaths, births, and marriages were rarely recorded in the 1910's, and neither the Charlevoix nor the Emmet county Courthouse has any records about Prudence Bolton. If Ernest Hemingway did know about Prudence's death he did not incorporate it into either of his two "Prudence" stories.

*   *   *

In 1974 several people in northern Michigan received the following letter from a woman living in Chicago. This letter raised many questions and caused a great deal of controversy among scholars who knew of its existence. The letter is included in its entirety here for the first time in a published text. The author of this letter could never be the daughter of Ernest Hemingway and Prudence Bolton, because Prudence Bolton died before the claimed birth of the letter writer who will remain anonymous. The entire letter is included as follows.

8/24/74

Dear Friend:

Pls. Excuse any typing errors as I type by hand as in 6/69, I became crippled from injuries to my left arm & hand,) which half amputated the left elbow, so I only have ltd . use of it all, since.

WE (I & husband) are only "little people of a

*poorer working class" here & I am almost 56 yrs;
he is 60 yrs.old, so we cant afford trips to your
area, for research, or for even a vacation, at this
time, & we both have been ill, too. Thus, we are
obliged to work by mail , & ask your aid. We also
cant afford costly detectives or genealogists, but I
can afford a modest fee for your Xerox of any facts
& photos you can locate, to help us.*

*I am adopted & serious trouble has come upon
us, here—over my real "Identity", so I urgently need
my original papers, etc. & I now narrowed down
my real parent's courtship days & perhaps my real
birthplace—to your Emmet Cty. Area of Petoskey
& Walloon Lake, Mich. Of course, I would like to
come to see you personally, & maybe can do so,
someday, but for now, I need facts you have, to aid
me-by mail-for vital files here, re it all not to do
with any inheritance but with U.S. Immigration
and Govt, etc.*

1.   *I am the illegitimate daughter of Ernest Miller
     Hemingway, & he was born in our suburb of
     Oak Pk. Ill. & often was in & lived then
     after WW1, as a youth—in Chg. too, AND
     Prudence (Trudy) Boulton, whom he knew
     from their childhood days-UP IN
     MICHIGAN. She was 2 yrs. Younger than
     Ernest & she was part French, part Ottawa
     Indian, with some English blood (many
     Boulton families of England-then into
     Canada, were of high families-& Govt. Ofls.
     kin to Royalty, etc.). She was pretty, perhaps
     5'4", looked white-with fair skin & lovely
     long black hair. In 1910, she & Ernest both
     attended your Resort 11 school-a 1 room type,*

*as too, his Hemingway family—from this
area—since 1899, went all summers, into
fall—to their "Windemere" summer farm-
estate-cottage-home, at Walloon Lake, Mich.
In Emmet Cty. So Ernest grew up with your
Indians (Ottawa & Chippewas), & fished,
hunted with them—played as a child with
their children, spoke some Indian languages,
knew their parents, etc. The Indians he knew-
they lived in the poor type Indian Camp in
shacks, near to his summer farm & home of
"Windemere"—now a Natl. Historic Site,
since 1968, via U.S. Dept. of Interior-which
handles Indian Affairs, too. So, young
Prudence—who became the beloved TRUDY
(the FIRST & ONLY REAL LOVE of Ernest
Hemingway)—lived with her father, a widower
it seems—Richard (Nick) Boulton—a tall,
part French, part Ottawa Indian, with some
English blood, who looked white & orig. was
from Canada, of a fur trader family of Indians
there—in a poor shack in the Indian Camp.
Ernest wanted to marry Trudy, when in 1917
she was 15 yrs. Old & he then was a tall, lean,
handsome, brunette-French Count type (he was
part French, part English) & was 17 yrs. old,
but his RICH & POWERFUL FAMILY
objected, to a marriage of "their son" with a
"mere, poor little half breed".*

2.   *Trudy was a Catholic, so maybe went to an
     Indian Cath. Church in your area, which
     has some files on her birth, & death & my
     birth??? & maybe some early school. & Local
     health board, & vital statistics files &*

historical, & civic, etc files of yours, can aid me?

3.   *Ernest was very close to NICK & HER (father & daughter-his Indian pals) so he even, later, named his eldest son (whom I say is adopted & that his 3 sons are & that I am the only child of Ernest Hemingway—due too, to the horrible WWI war wounds he got in Italy, in 1918—"John NICKANER (Nick & Her— & in memory, eh?) Hemingway"—who 1923 was born in Toronto, Canada) & NICK sometimes found odd jobs as a carpenter etc. at a Saw Mill in your area then in early 1900s-up to 1913. The mother of Prudence Boulton was Annie Tabasach, (Boulton) & the Boulton family had Indian kin & pals named Mitchell, Taylor, & Tabasah—in your Emmet Cty. Area & Petoskey, etc.—then . . . Ernest also knew Rich White Families he went with, or dated their daughters, of your area—summers as a Goldstein, Connable, Griffin, Pailthorp, Rosenthal, Bump—so if any of these still live in your area summers or all yr. Maybe they recall facts on my real mother, especially & re myself born Sept.8, 1918.*

4.   *Ernest's family were devout Prots. Of a Congregationalist Church—i.e. of his father, but his mother was an Episcopalian, so maybe some members or ofls. Of these—in your area, whom you may know, could recall any facts re my real mother, etc. to assist me to trace my birth & adoption, etc.??*

5.   *His father was the Rich, Prominent, Socially*
     High, DR CLARENCE EDMUNDS (or
     Edmonds) HEMINGWAY, born in Oak Park.
     Ill. A doctor—M.D.) Obstetrician—so he
     aided ill Indians & delivered their babies, in
     your area, summers & into fall—when he
     was at his "Windemere" estate-farm-home; &
     as I was born in fall—Sept. 8, 1918, he—
     my own Grandfather—could have delivered
     me to Trudy Boulton, "at home" in her poor
     shack in the Indian camp near his estate-
     farm, etc. at Walloon lake, Mich. In Emmet
     Cty. As too, Dr C Hemingway has safely
     delivered "at home" in his lovely house-now
     also a Natl. Historic Site—in Oak Pk. Ill.
     His own six children, of four daughters &
     two sons—including Ernest—his first &
     oldest son-born to him & his wife, Mrs. Grace
     Hall Hemingway—July 21, 1899. So, would
     not some local Health Dept. or Medical Files
     of yours show my birth, if I was born in your
     area, 9/8/1918; plus show then or soon after-
     the sad death of my young, 16 yrs. old unwed
     mother-Trudy Boulton, of Childbirth
     Complications? I need too-name of the doctor
     attending her at my birth & her death; of
     the Priest for her funeral; of her cemetery, so
     maybe your local Coroner or Police or Potters
     field for paupers KNOW her cemetery so I can
     send her some flowers too, from me, for her
     grave-with its simple Cross. I was named
     Fredericka Adeleide. Ernest was dying in Italy
     of war wounds from Germans, at my birth-
     when he turned Catholic then-as too, Trudy
     died at my birth-when & I suppose his pals of

*your area wrote him to the Milan Milit. Hosp.
All about IT, too, (UP IN MIC. Eh?) Then at
my adoption, it got changed to Florence
(Ernest was in Italy as is city of Florence in 9/
1918-when I was born) Adelaide (after my
Great Grandmother ADELAIDE Edmunds
Hemingway-mother of his father DR. C.
HEMINGWAY-wife of Grandfather of Ernest-
in Oak Pk. Too in 1918—often the RICH
POWERFUL: ATTY. AARON or ANSON
TYLER HEMINGWAY-whose father was
ALLEN HEMINGWAY, a POSTMASTER
IN CONN. About 1844. My adopting family
too, were orig. from Conn. & England, France,
Germany like the Hemingways & Hall-of
Ernest' family & were interwed & they
adopted me in PA. For the HEMINGWAYS-
their Kin. So I was raised as JEWISH by them
in Scranton, Pa., but both my real parents of
Ernest & Trudy were Catholics, so I was sent
awhile to a Convent to study art, etc. under
Nuns, in Pa. & Priests often at our homes,
etc . . . but, of course—an illegit. Baby born
back in 1918 was this "awful scandal &
disgrace" (not so much now eh?) that could
TOTALLY RUIN THE PATERNAL &
MATERNAL FAMILIES THEN, especially
if one was RICH & POWERFUL like the
HEMINGWAYS, as too my Great
GRANTFATHER-ATTY   ANSON
HEMINGWAY was a devout Christian. Like
his wife, ADELAIDE EDMUNDS
HEMINGWAY—my Great Grandmother &
whom I am named after—of a strict PROT.
Type & were CIVIC LEADERS in Oak Pk.*

Ill. Plus he had his LAW ofc. In CHO. & he was for awhile the EXEC. DIR.Secr. OF OUR metropolitan YMCA of CGO. & he knew here, such RICH, POWERFUL MEN as JOE MEDILL: MAYOR OF CHO; then his hero grandson, COL. ROBT. McCormick (Owners of CGO. TRIBUNE) & their kin—CYRUS McCORMICK of reaper family— MILLIONAIRES & Potter PALMER (Hotel Owners) & Marshall FIELD, etc.

My dear late adopting mother closely resembled GRACE HALL HEMINGWAY, in facial features, traits, ideas; both with kin in Conn. & seem cousins; while she too, seems a distant kin to her husband, my dear adopting father—in Scranton, Pa, and he was TALL—6' or so, like my PAPA (Ernest Hemingway) & my Grandpa—Nick Boulton of Mich; & was 15 yrs. Older than Ernest & was also lean, a handsome brunette who looked like a tall FRENCH COUNT closely resembled both Ernest & his father, Dr. Clarence E. Hemingway! Too, my real & adopting Families are both a Great type—of thus SCIENTISTS; GOVT. OFLS. HERE; KIN TO ROYALTY; DOCTORS; LAWYERS;ARTISTS; PROFL.MUSICIANS; WRITERS, etc. (I did profit. Writing here too in past yrs. . . .).

6.   *So my adopting parents in 1921 when they adopted me (I first lived in Brooklyn, NY, as a baby & recall it & Grandparents of Ernest had kin in NY State as had my adopting*

*parents) were VERY RICH, too-but lost it all
in Depression, so I am poor since . . . & I lived
here, for better jobs, etc. for to 30 yrs. Now (&
WE are reputable)*

7. *So, comes now—it is 1917 & little, pretty 15
    yr. old Prudence (Trudy) Boulton is very poor
    & lives in a poor shack in the Indian Camp
    near the lovely HEMINGWAY summer farm-
    cottage-home-estate aka "Windemere" in
    Emmet Cty. At Walloon Lake, Mich.—with
    her kindly, friendly widowed father aka
    NICK Boulton—a well known father & his
    cherished young daughter COUPLE—as the
    both get this "swell jobs offer" from their long
    time friends—the RICH, PROMINENT,
    WHITES—HEMINGWAY Family—which
    both the poor Boultons need badly, for food &
    clothes, being "just Indians." IT was as a
    little (15 yrs. Old) servant-maid-cook-little
    mommie type-housekeeper, in the lovely
    HEMINGWAY cottage home, to aid Mrs.
    Grace Ernestina (my adopting mother was
    Sadie Ernestina—& both had TWINS in
    their mutual Families; both were wonderful
    CONCERT PIANISTS; both with some
    German blood)—Hall Hemingway, as
    GRACE—my grandmother—was actually
    "Far ahead of her Time" & sadly, poor
    GRACE—should have lived NOW in the time
    capsule of LIBERATED, WOMEN here—as
    she was a tragic FRUSTRATED CAREER
    WOMAN, who never belonged in life—as the
    prim, devout wife of a prominent doctor, with
    her sole function being to have babies & raise*

them & only doing civic or church duties—
a la the Early & Prim & "Kept Back in
every way PILGRIM WOMEN over here." As
GRACE was highly gifted, as an OPERA
SINGER, SINGING TEACHER & sang thus
in church choirs in Cgo. Too; & had studied
her adored MUSIC IN EUROPE being from a
VERY RICH FAMILY in Oak Pk. Ill. Of
ERNEST HALL (with some German, some
English blood), Plus, GRACE was a
wonderful ARTIST; PORTRAIT PAINTER
(I inherited THIS so growing up in Scranton,
Pa. I was always at my easel, too—painting
marvelous portraits, in her same style, plus I
was always a Poet & Writer too—in same
style of my real PAPA—Ernest Hemingway—
her son), plus GRACE was a wonderful concert
pianist (as was my dear adopting mother in
Pa.—her KIN—even resembled Grace . . .) so
GRACE had so much SOCIAL VALUE;
THRILLING MUSICAL & ARTISTIC
GIFTS, to give the world-that had she lived
NOW—she probably have remained single or
wed much as the fascinating CONCERT &
ORCHESRTRA CONDUCTOR &
LEADER in NYC or CGO. Or in PARIS,
France; & traveled with him-having no kids
or one—brought up by a tutor &
Nursemaids—as GRACE was no homemaker
or mother type (nor am I). She hated raising
children, being a non-domestic but a
CAREER type-her right to be WHAT SHE
WAS eh? As GOD MADE WOMEN FOR
CAREERS, too—not just mothers & maid
types for husbands-men;

8. *Instead, after studying in NYC at the Opera & in EUROPE as in glamorous PARIS (how are you gonna keep them down on the farm after seen PAREE"???)—& longing to become another female CAROUSO or another MADAM GALIA KERCHEE etc. & knowing the thrill of facing an AUDIENCE from the STAGE (no biz like SHOW BIZ.), poor GRACE— was really "forced" by her strict, devout Episcopalian father—RICH, PROMINENT ERNEST HALL of Oak Park, & Cgo, Ill—to "forget all this career nonsense of being a SINGER & OPERA & or CONCERT PIANIST(as in Palaces of KINGS & in London-Paris—) or ARTIST (as for PRESIDENTS & Magazine covers— this FAMOUS ILLUSTRATOR)—& settle down-to being a good wife & mother as this is all a girl or woman is intended for—to marry a nice young man & to raise (& bear) his children & go to church & stop this nonsense & folly!"*

9. *So, we find the Oak Pk. Ill HEMINGWAY home a MESS—with boxes around, & DR. C. HEMINGWAY is doing the housework, as wife GRACE is busy painting portraits; singing; concert playing—thru Litz (sic), Bach, Behoven (sic) (my adopting mother, too! All day with THE MASTERS at her Concert Piano in our Scranton, Pa. Home)— but WONDERFUL MUSIC a la STRAVINSKY style—as in PALACE OF CZAR NICK OF RUSSIA—prior 1918 . . .*

10. *So comes "Windemere" & long suffering DR.
C. HEMINGWAY—my good grandfather—
but not Intellectual—a strict, very devout
Prot. Type (Congreg.) devoted father, good
husband—waited on his wife; put up with
her 3 fold careers & her lack of Domestic
abilities; but aside from being Doctor to RICH
WHITES & POOR INDIANS in MICH. He
loves Hunting & fishing, too! But where HE
had to be both father & mother to his six
children, at "WINDEMERE" AS IN Oak Pk.
ILL. Plus THERE—the maid, cook,
homemaker, etc. he had no time at all to enjoy
HIS LIFE too—for a change! At fishing,
hunting—all he loved, as did his oldest son,
Ernest Hemingway—*

11. *So, DR.C.HEMINGWAY found a swell
solution to his domestic problems, so he hired
young 15 yrs. old Prudence Boulton
(TRUDY), whom Ernest & his whole family
knew, as mentioned, for yrs.—in your area of
Emmet Cty. & of Petoskey, Mich.—as a little
mommie, i.e. as a servant maid, cook,
affection giver, family greeter, housekeeper—
part time (she then slept in her shack, as did
her kindly father, NICK Boulton) and Dr. C.
Hemingway also then hired her father NICK
as his own part time jobs man & carpenter.
So TRUDY aided GRACE (MRS)
HEMINGWAY in the home—while her
father NICK aided Dr. Hemingway around
the cottage home, farm & in carpenter work.
Thus NICK & HER became Members of the
HEMINGWAY household*

12. *Parties went on, for Ernest & his family there,
as for Christmas of 1917—why not? A
horrible WAR—over there-was grimly nearing
OUR SHORES—& maybe there would be NO
TOMORROW for of us—so, too-from Dec.
1917 to Sept. 1918 is 9 months (I was born
Set. 8, 1918—). But GOD has a purpose in
ALL HE DOES & I have just as much right
being here as does any other American, plus
"i" am "the LEGACY of ERNST
HEMINGWAY—TO HIS COUNTRY"—*

13. *So, suddenly in Jan. 1918, Ernest got rushed
off scene in Mich. (ohh, Trudy was then 1
month pregnant & it was learned, eh?? By
all up there UP IN MICHIGAN as per stories
made famous later by ERNEST, plus I am in
his famous FAREWELL TO ARMS &
LOVE) re UP IN MICH. Days but set in Italy
& I am his baby in IT—lost forever to him,
eh???) For a small job as a cub reporter—his
first WRITING break, so he grabbed it—for
the KANSAS CITY STAR in MO.—which
his RICH, POWERFUL FAMILY got for him
via JUDGES etc. there knew THERE. . . . so
he wrote for them . . . went out on Police,
Hospital, Health emergencies, Assault
CASES—from Jan. 1918 to April, 1918.
Ernest sadly was rejected for U.S. ARMY
MILITARY Service which grieved him badly,
as his ancestors (& mine thus) were brave
SOLDIERS at VALLEY FORGE, PA. (my
home area, eh? Adopted there) in CONTL.
ARMY; in our CIVIL WAR in UNION
ARMY—on our HEMINGWAY side. Due to*

*a bad eye-rather weak, as prior to his birth,
his mother GRACE once had scarlet fever
which affected her eyes, so she then wore
glasses; & Ernest inherited a weakness in 1
eye, too, at his birth to her. But to his
happiness, Ernest got accepted in 4/18 as
an   AMERICAN   RED   CROSS
AMBULANCE DRIVER so he proudly sailed
from NYC—then being 18 yrs. old
(TRUDY—still in MICH. In your area, was
then 16 yrs. old) to Paris—then into ITALY
(Where he then fought too with the ITALIAN
ARMY & became one of our Greatest WWI
WAR HEROS (then in WWII for US, too &
later he became one of the WORLD'S MOST
FAMOUS WRITER) some say, in his time—
he was then OUR GREATEST AMERICAN
WRITER—always fought for Social Justice
& Civil Rights & defended US—the Little
People—so he wrote thus about his pals—
waitresses, bartenders, poor Indians; as he
scorned the RICH, HYPOCRITES he had
met—so empty & selfish.*

14. *so TRUDY died at my birth or soon after &
all UP IN MICH. Knew "her baby was the
child of ERNEST HEMINGWAY'—then
NICK father VANISHED, too—so did he die
in 1918 too & of WHAT? An ailment—a
strange "hunting accident" or ??I then got
whisked off for adoption by Jewish kin of my
Hemingway real family as too, our ancestor,
a brave 17 yrs. old HERO of AMER. REVOL.
In 1776 at Concord, Lexington & Valley
Forge, Pa. Was CORPORAL JACOB*

HEMINGSTEIN, the ERNEST HEMINGWAY of his day! A young, brave, German Jew! Who came over here, to escape the social & religious tyranny & persecution in PRUSSIA ALL EUROPE then—in 1700s—so over here, he found IT here, too, eh? As no one HERE then dared to be a thing except—ANGLO SAXON or ENGLISH, WHITE & PROT. I.e. IF you expected to get a job, & "be approved of by your neighbors" thus no one could admit OVER HERE & into 1800s & STILL in some areas of "AMERICA" to being Catholic, Irish, Italian, Jewish, Black, Indian (Amer.), German background, Japanese background, etc. as the "only REAL Americans were always & only ENGLISH, WHITE & PROT. Eh? Thus young, courageous, intelligent JACOB HEMINGSTEIN inter wed—& changed his name to HEMINGWAY so thus became "the only REAL American" eh? (WOTTA JOKE ABOUT THIS BEING ANY free nation with equality; OPPORTUNITY; RIGHTS; LIBERTIES; JUSTICE FOR ALL, in or out of Courts—as too, helpless, poorer class, little people have not had a COUNTRY or any such rights, since 1776 or still; WE cant even WIN a suit here-due to the crooked, selfish, pd. off JUDGES, who always FAVOR the RICHER Party, eh?) SO:

15. *My maternal kin include CHIEF PETOSAEGA, who once owned much of your area & after whom your PETOSKEY is named (means: THE RISING SUN as re BOOK by*

my PAPA THE SUN ALSO RISESS;) CHIEF ANDREW JACKSON BLACK BIRD, the POSTMASTER in your N. MICH. In late 1800s & he, too, was a WRITER so see libraries re HIS BOOKS, too . . .

16. *SO, I need your aid, from any old FILES or RECOLLECTIONS of yourself or of anyone you know of Emmet Cty. & Petoskey& your Walloon Lake, Mich. area on:*

A. Any birth, schooling, death FILES on Prudence Boulton, my real mother? And her cemetery address.

B. Any birth & adoption FILES or FACTS on MYSELF (born Sept. 8, 1918 (where?) to her & Ernest Hemingway?

C. Any FILE on the Death of her father– my maternal Grandfather-NICK (Richard) Boulton; or did he move back to Canada or if a grave exists for him, too, in 1918-the address of his Cemetery (near to "WINDEMERE"/ as is grave of little TRUDY Boulton??); any Baptismal file on ME in any Cath. Or Indian Cath. Church or census roll of your area? Any photo of TRUDY & NICK?? (NICK & HER) for ME? I have of all the HEMINGWAYS & their facts.

Ernest KNEW well the Ralph CONNABLE & the Dutch PAILTHORP Families in your area then in 1917-18 (they were from Cgo. & Ill. Too) so if any of them still are in Petoskey or area, do they KNOW of NICK Boulton died; moved away; was SLAIN or?? As too—by the "sudden DEATH in Sept. 1918 of both NICK & HER (Trudy)

*BOULTON & when my PAPA (Ernest) was
dying in Italy in WWI—meant that "this
horrible scandal created by my illegit. Birth—
to the HEMINGWAYS-would be forever SI-
LENCED, WIPED OUT by such VANISH-
ING of NICK & HER; & my adoption FAR
FROM NK MICH. eh" ?? But GOD has
HIS OWN PLANS so this—thru me, his only
daughter, my PAPA (Ernest) WRITES
AGAIN—in this request to all of you, UP IN
HIS BELOVED MICH. to aid me. FOR him,
if you can? Thank you.*

An elderly woman, who wishes to remain anonymous, gave me this letter. She had some thoughts that she shared with me. Her first question was why did the writer of this letter wait until she was fifty-six years old to find out whether she was Ernest Hemingway's daughter? My informer also felt that the letter writer received most of her information from Carlos Baker's biography.

But Prudence Bolton could not have given birth to the writer of this letter in September 1918, since Prudence died on February 15, 1918, seven months before. The letter writer also does not give the names of her adoptive parents, except to say that her mother's name was Sadie Ernestina. She does hint that her adoptive mother resembled Ernest's mother, so that there might be a family relationship.

This overly discussed letter shows a great deal of research by the writer and might be a source of inquiry for future scholars. But the date of Prudence Bolton's death precludes the birth of the letter writer, but still leaves open the possibility of the three month's old fetus of Prudence Bolton being the child of Ernest Hemingway.

Chapter IV

HARBOR POINT

Earlier when Woody picked up the dress for Mrs. Fay from the girl who looked like May Ling, he felt hopeful for the first time, since he heard that May Ling was missing. In a strange way he felt as if now he had a second chance.

Since he had been back in the States he could not focus on anything. Everything seemed dry and shallow, and he had the sense that his life was over. He was only twenty-five, but he had been on his own since his father died, and his mother had sent him to boarding school. He was the smallest kid at the school when the family chauffeur drove him East and dropped him off at Avon Old Farms. Woody used his wits to outsmart the senior bullies and earned a reputation as a scrapper. But he only felt alive and in control of his life now when he was flying a plane. Sometimes he woke up with night sweats, and he felt so wound up that he could spin out of control. He knew that he needed a woman. His own woman. Like May Ling.

Woody decided to fly the floatplane back to the airport and drove his fire engine red Olds convertible back to the Point parking garages. He jumped on a bike he kept in the garage and rode on the interior road that passed by the back end of the Harbor Point cottages. One belonged to a U.S. Senator. Another belonged to the former wife of the brother of the President. The names were the household names of the major corporations of the Midwest. The fortunes came from Procter and Gamble, Pullman railroad cars, and numerous banks, law firms, and manufacturing companies. Woody was anchored in the Grosse Pointe crowd which had interlocking directorships, which were called marriages, and lifelong friendships with the other groups from St. Louis, Cincinnati, Lake Forest, Louisville, Locust Valley, San Francisco, and Kansas City. Since Detroit was the closest major city and the automotive fortunes were the newest, the Grosse Pointe crowd, which was in truth the flashiest and most flamboyant, was considered a "little nouvue-riche." Woody didn't give a damn.

He pulled his bike up to the back entrance of the Fay cottage which was a thirty-five room log cabin facing out on the Lake Michigan side of Harbor Point. He ran up the several flights of stairs through the pines on the hill where the cottage was perched, not bothering to use the tram the Fays built. He dropped the dress off with a maid at the back door and escaped before Bitsy or Mrs. Fay saw him. He felt fourteen again as he pedaled furiously away on his bicycle.

The Woodward cottage was near the end of Harbor Point, five houses from the lighthouse. One of the white frame with green shutters mansion-cottages, it had porches on both the harbor and lakeside. Tuberous begonias spilled in early summer orange and red profusion from the window boxes on both porches. The three-story cottage was symmetrical with screened-in sleeping porches, which had been occupied by hay fever sufferers for three or four generations.

As Woody burst into the blue-and-white chintz covered living room like the teenager he felt he was, he ran into his mother. They avoided each other and usually only met at strained dinner hours. Lucretia Francis Jones Woodward Carlton Greer was on her way to make another drink when Woody threw open the door.

"God, Woody!" She tipped a little as she walked.

Woody's good mood began sinking as he looked at his mother in her white linen dress, Bob Baker shoes, and tightly curled bleached blonde hair. He braced himself for the first criticism.

"Where have you been? The Jones' cocktail party begins in fifteen minutes."

"I'm not going."

"Woody. You have to go. Your stepfather isn't here, and you must escort me."

"I don't want to go. Go by yourself. It is only three doors down. God, mother, you're capable of walking that far. But maybe not."

"Don't be rude, Woody. You are just like your father. Unruly."

"Come on, mother."

"No, go upstairs immediately and take a shower and change."

"I told you. I'm not going."

Lucretia, or Letty, as everyone called her, dropped onto the couch and took a long sip of her drink while looking at Woody under her hooded eyelids. He had inherited her eyes, but now hers were bleary and unfocused, while his were going from side to side, looking for a way out.

"Woody, I think the least you could do is take me to one little cocktail party after all I have done for you."

Woody felt cornered, trapped, as he always did in his mother's presence. He did not mind being with her in the morning, but when she had too much to drink by late afternoon, he avoided her. Then he thought of the perfect out.

"Mother, I'm going with Bitsy Fay to dinner with her parents at the club." He felt that he has escaped one trap for another, but it was the lesser of two evils.

"Oh." Letty Greer sat up. "You are joining the Fays at the Club?" She had encouraged his friendship with the cute, little Fay girl. Maybe she can settle him down, and she certainly isn't after his money, Letty thought.

"Yes. That's right. Gotta go." And Woody ran upstairs and waited in his room until his mother tottered down the stairs and then down the sidewalk to the cocktail party. Then Woody felt free to come downstairs, and fix himself a drink. He went out to the porch on the lakeside and watched the white caps out on Lake Michigan. He took a little time to himself, as he stared at the bright afternoon sun on the water and watched the birds follow the wind currents. He sniffed the breeze and figured out the wind currents just as the birds did.

Then he thought of May Ling, and this new girl

he had just met, and his eccentric father who he still missed daily after eleven years, and wondered what he was going to do with the rest of his life. Another two million had been put into his hands from the trust fund on his twenty-fifth birthday on February seventh. He didn't have to work, if he didn't feel like it. But after living on the edge for the last six years, he needed something. Maybe he would start his own airline?

The telephone rang, and Joseph, the butler, came to get him.

"Miss Fay, sir," he said, as he handed Woody the inside phone with the long extension cord.

"Hi, Bitsy. What's up?" He monotoned. "Okay. I'll pick you up in an hour."

*   *   *

The Fay family held the most important table at the Little Harbor Club. Just like the tables at El Morocco in the Fifties, you knew who was who at the Little Harbor Club by where you sat, and the Little Harbor Club did not have a maitre d' that you could bribe for a better seat to avoid "Siberia." In the pecking order the Fays were the top in both categories of rank: money and breeding. Both Mr. And Mrs. Fay were descended from the original white settlers of Harbor Point, and with his railroad family fortune merged with her banking fortune, they made the top of any list. The "A" party list began with the Fays.

Woody was seated in the place of honor on Mrs. Fay's right, and Bitsy was right next to him. Mrs. Fay knew that according to protocol Bitsy should have been on the other side of the family table next to old Mr. Webb, but she could not risk any other woman next to Woody so early in the game. She was thinking that a nice white winter wedding might be workable.

Woody felt like a hunting trophy bagged by Bitsy and Mrs. Fay and shown off for all to see at the Little Harbor Club dance. He wore his blue blazer, button down shirt, regimental tie, and yellow pants. Mr. Fay was wearing his Madras jacket and red pants which clashed with Mrs. Fay's coral chiffon dress. At the Little Harbor Club, as in Palm Beach, the male of the species was decked out in more colorful plumage than the females. All of the gray, brown, and dark blue uniforms of the work world were left behind for a rainbow of primary colors.

"Now, Woody," Mrs. Fay began, "Are you planning to stay all summer?"

"Probably."

"Do you have a job in the fall?"

"No."

"What do you plan to do?"

"Mummy," cautioned Bitsy.

Woody's eyes started looking around the room. He was getting claustrophobic, and the first course had not even arrived.

"Now, Woody, what is it you plan to do?" Mrs. Fay continued her line of questioning.

"Get a drink," said Woody, jumping to his feet and running downstairs to the bar before Bitsy followed him. He ducked into the men's room just to make sure she could not catch him. When he was sure that she was not outside, he went down the hall to the bar.

The downstairs bar looked like a set from "Casablanca" down to the paddle fans. The walls were covered with reeds, and the furniture was rattan. Woody felt comfortable here. It reminded him of Indochina. Cliff and Joyce were the bartender and the barmaid. Cliff looked like Clark Gable, and she looked like Lauren Bacall. They were married. They lived in Palm Springs, and the Philippine club manager, Jose, brought them north with him each May.

"So Woody, how's it going?" Cliff began pouring him a bourbon and soda. Cliff knew what everyone at the Club drank.

"Can't complain. Got any Camels?"

"What's up? You don't smoke." Said Cliff passing him the cigarettes with one hand and writing up his bar tab with the other.

"I need them tonight."

"Sure."

"I'm at the Fay table."

"Have another pack," Cliff laughed.

"The old lady is cross examining me. I escaped down here."

"What is she asking?"

"What I intend to do to become eligible to be her son-in-law."

"Moving fast?"

"Speed of light."

"Bitsy?"

"Uh-huh."

"A little soon."

"You're telling me. I better get back before they start tracking me down."

"See you later. Good luck."

"I'll need it."

When Woody returned, the first course was on the table. Mrs. Fay had turned her attention on Billy Belcher, the Palm Beach sportsman whom she was working on to get the Fays into the Bath and Tennis Club in Palm Beach.

Woody slid into his seat next to Bitsy without attracting Mrs. Fay's attention. He began tearing the Maine lobster apart which had arrived that afternoon by bus at Sault Saint Marie and had been picked up by one of Jose's underlinings. Woody always felt a little uneasy eating lobster with their beady dead eyes looking at him as he pulled off their claws. He did not like to hunt or fish or kill animals. In Bangkok they kidded him about being a Buddhist. He turned the head over, so that it was not accusing him of tearing off its legs and cracking them with the shell cracker.

"You do that *so* well," Bitsy cooed.

"Sure."

"No. You do. Most men make such a mess."

"I'm making a mess."

"Oh, Woody. Let me give you a compliment."

"I don't need compliments."

Bitsy fell silent and started to pout. Woody was glad that he did not have to talk to her.

The orchestra began playing Cole Porter and Rogers and Hammerstein tunes. The only way a Jew would enter the club was through their music, Ambrose Pierce made sure of that. The Little Harbor Club was the most expensive club in the United States, if you counted it by the days that it was open. They kept assessing the members for renovations of the club and rebuilding the swimming pool.

"Woody, let's dance."

"I haven't had dessert yet."

"You don't like desserts."

"Tonight I do."

A young blonde man took away the lobster shell and brought a baked Alaska.

"You enjoy waiting here?" Woody asked.

"Yes, sir."

"What's your name?"

"Roger, sir."

"Roger what?"

"Roger Wisniewski, sir."

"Where are you from, Roger?"

"Lansing."

"Go to Michigan State?"

"Yes, sir."

"Good basketball team."

"Yes, sir," said Roger Wisniewski thankful to be treated like a human being, not like the servant that most of them treated him as. He finished cleaning their table.

"Woody, do you have to always talk to the help?"

"That kid could probably run circles around both of us academically. He's a college kid, what do you mean 'help'?"

"Like with Cliff and Joyce."

"They're my friends. You are a little snob." He got up to go down to the bar. "I think I'll go down and see them now."

When Woody entered the downstairs bar, it was beginning to fill up. Many of the younger members had the same idea he did and drifted downstairs. The younger crowd ran from fifteen from Bitsy's younger sister and the precocious Smith twins, also fifteen, to Woody, the oldest at twenty-five. None of them worked, and many would never hold a real job. Many of the males went to Ivy League colleges. Most of the men would go into their family business, a few would go into professions, or some would start small businesses of their own. The women would try to marry well.

"So, Woody escaped again," Cliff laughed.

"Just in the nick of time."

"Don't let them pressure you."

"Don't worry. No one traps me."

"Hey, Woody, give me a ride in your plane sometime?" asked Derek Haswell, the wilder Haswell twin. Jeff and Derek were fraternal twins, seventeen, from New York, and were not alike in any way. While Derek was tall and masculine, Jeff was shorter, fatter, and looked like a cherub. He was anything but cherubic in nature and had thoughts more like those of Fatty Arbuckle.

Woody liked Derek and had assumed an older brother role with him. The Haswell house, which was Victorian with turrets, was next to the Woodward cottage on the Point. Of the entire younger group that was always in the Little Harbor Club bar, Derek was the one most similar to Woody. Derek had filled Woody in on the Fay girls and their games.

"Sure, anytime. How about tomorrow?"

"I have a race at 1:30," said Derek.

"What kind?"

"Marlins." The Marlin racing class was the training ground in the sailboat competitions for teenagers under eighteen. At eighteen they moved up to their father's and uncle's sleek class of "Northern Michigans," a unique class of thirty-three foot wooden boats, which only raced at Harbor Springs and Charlevoix. Northern Michigans, or NM's, were smaller versions of the America's Cup sailboats.

"I used to race Marlins."

"Yeah, I heard you were something."

"Maybe."

"Why don't you have a N.M.?"

"I'd rather fly. And besides I lost all those years of racing."

At that moment Debbie Smith, one of the fifteen-year-old Smith twins, came up and pressed herself against Derek. He flushed and tucked her under his arm where she looked up at him boldly. The Smith twins were not that pretty with their carrot hair and freckled big heads, but they were loud, sexy, and outrageous.

"So-o-o, Derek, gonna dance with me?"

"Gonna do more than dance with you," he squeezed her.

"Promises, promises."

Woody ordered another drink.

"So Woody Woodpecker," said Debbie from the safety of Derek's armpit.

"Yes," Woody turned his pale eyes directly on her.

"So you're quite the flyer."

"Maybe."

"With Bitsy?"

"Maybe."

"Come on, Derek. Let's dance."

Woody followed them upstairs.

The only table, which had anywhere near the important position of the Fay's, was E.J. MacCloud's table. A nouvue-riche newcomer, E.J. was not only new money, but he was a local, born in a poor neighborhood of Petoskey across the bay. E.J. had made his fortune in several schemes from car dealerships to sales and advertising gimmicks. He was good at stealing others' ideas, using them as his own, and selling himself. E.J. could sell anything, but selling himself was his greatest triumph. The selling of E.J. MacCloud was a hard sell from any standpoint. He was short, grossly overweight, and looked like Porky

Pig. He only graduated from Petoskey High and used ungrammatical English. But he had a driving ambition comparable to that of Jay Gatsby and wanted his Great Lakes yacht as much as Gatsby. Now with a fortune from Scotch Stamps, a rival to Green Stamps, he used a company airplane, yacht, and summerhouse as his own private possessions. His business partner, the also short, penny-pinching German, A.J. Schiller, was an easy target for a slow and insidious takeover. MacCloud landed on the Schiller business doorstep at twenty and through flattery and manipulation had gained almost complete control of the family company of A. Schiller and Sons. MacCloud was successful in driving out the two sons and was ready to eliminate the paterfamilias and take the company public. Old Schiller had always trusted the serpent, MacCloud, over the advice of his wife and his two sons, which he drove from the family business garden of Eden.

E.J. MacCloud ate his third baked Alaska and stared at the Fay table. The Fay's dinner guests were all well dressed and old guard while his were all hangers-on employee sycophants. They were loud and overdressed. E.J.'s little pig eyes lighted on Woody. He alerted his company pilot, Jack Du Barry, who had flown President Hoover's plane. Jack was dashing in a World War II aviator way and always served as an extra man at night for E.J after flying during the day.

"Jack, know that kid?"

"Which one?"

"The one sitting down on Mrs. Fay's right."

"Nope."

"He's a pilot."

"Commercial?"

"Ain't sure, but heard he flew in the Berlin airlift and Dien Bien Phu."

"Good stuff."

"Next time he goes to the bar, follow him and introduce yourself."

"What for?"

"Maybe use him as copilot."

"Okay. Will do."

At the moment the Smith twins came dancing out on the floor together. The orchestra picked up the beat even though they had planned a break. Everyone else had left the dance floor. The women started whispering to each other about Lila Smith's redheaded girls and their increasingly outrageous behavior. The twins looked impishly at everyone to make sure that they were the center of attention, and then they coyly started pulling up their demure dresses, which their mother had picked out for them. A hush fell over the parents. Had the Smith twins had too much to drink? Emmet Thurston began to move out on the dance floor to stop them. He thought maybe they did not have any underpants on. The Smith girls watched Emmet approach and twirled beyond his reach. They danced sideways, stopped, lifted their skirts, went bottoms up, and exposed ruffled pantaloons. The mothers sighed with relief, but still were shocked. The Smith twin's high jinks were going too far. They were becoming a bad influence on the other teenage girls.

"I've had enough," said Woody grabbing Bitsy's arm, thanking Mrs. Fay, and getting to his feet. "I need to get down to the Pier Bar."

"Oh, Woody, you're so dangerous," said Bitsy, glad that he wasn't impressed by the Smith twins antics.

She thought that they were to be watched. The Fay girls did not like to be upstaged.

When Woody entered the Pier Bar with its heavy smoke, beer smell, noise from the jukebox, and men yelling at each other, he felt more comfortable. He pulled off his coat and tie while he ushered Bitsy, her sisters, and their friends to an out-of-harms-way corner table.

As he waited at the end of the bar ordering drinks, he saw her again. May Ling dressed in Western clothes slinking across the room towards the bar. No, it's that other girl. What's her name? The local. Is she smiling at me? Oh, my god. She wants me. I will go over and talk to her. To hell with Bitsy and the group.

"Hello again," he said to her.

Chapter D

From "History of Northern Michigan," *Hemingway in Michigan,* pp. 11-19.

The history of northern Michigan embraces Indian wars, French and British occupation, frontier expansion, and the rough-and-tumble of lumbering days. A sense of this past was captured in Hemingway's Michigan writings—a past which Hemingway came to know, for he was a witness to the last years of the lumbering era. The Hemingway family lived each summer in a rough cottage, much as the first Michigan pioneers had lived before them. From his Indian friends he learned what it was to lead a frontier existence.

The Indians in northern Michigan encountered by Jean Nicolet, a French explorer who passed through the Straits of Mackinac in 1634, were of the same tribes

Hemingway knew more than two and a half centuries later, the Ottawas and Chippewas (the English name for the Indian word, Ojibwas), tribes of the Algonquin family. The place of origin of the Ottawas is obscure, but it is generally assumed that the tribe came from the east, advanced up the Ottawa River in Canada, then moved westward off the north shore of Lake Huron and passed by the Manitoulin Islands. At Sault Saint Marie they first met the Chippewas, who inhabited the country bordering on Lake Superior. The two tribes were surprised to find that, although neither had known of the existence of the other, their languages were so similar that they were able to converse. A loose confederacy was established between the Ottawas, Chippewas, and Potawatamis, and they became known as The Three Brothers. These tribes held undisputed possession of nearly the whole lower peninsula of Michigan.

In 1668 Father Jacques Marquette established the first permanent settlement in Michigan at the foot of the rapids on what is now the American side of the Sault Saint Marie. He was sent to New France to be a missionary among the Ottawas. An Indian war among the Sioux, the Hurons, and the Ottawas, in which the Sioux tribe was victorious, drove Father Marquette to Michilimackinac and finally to what was to be named St. Ignace. In 1671 he established a mission, named after St. Ignatius, which

was the first white settlement at the Straits
of Mackinac.

A letter written by Marquette in 1671
describes the region which Hemingway's
Nick Adams later passes through in the story
"Big Two-Hearted River."

> *Michilimackinac is an island, famous*
> *in these regions, of more than a league in*
> *diameter, elevated in some place by such high*
> *cliffs as to be seen more than twelve leagues*
> *off. It is situated just in the strait forming*
> *the communication between Lake Huron and*
> *Illinois* [Lake Michigan]. *It is the key and,*
> *as it were, the gate for all the tribes from the*
> *south, as the Sault is for those of the north,*
> *there being in this section of country only those*
> *two passages by water; for a great number of*
> *nations have to go by one or the other of these*
> *channels, in order to reach the French*
> *settlements.*

Father Marquette remained with the
mission at St. Ignace for about two years and
exercised control over the Indians living in
the area of northern Michigan where
Hemingway later lived. Marquette wanted
to explore the Mississippi and on May 17,
1673, left St. Ignace with the explorer Louis
Jolliet and five men. The co-discoverers of
the Mississippi followed it as far as what is
now Arkansas, determining that the river
must empty into the Gulf of Mexico.
Returning up the river, Father Marquette
was stricken with dysentery, from which he

had previously suffered; and fearing that he was going to die, he set out, from the present vicinity of Chicago, for St. Ignace.

On May 18, 1675, Father Marquette died at the age of thirty-eight—some scholars believe on the shore of what is now called the Betsie River in southern Michigan—hundreds of miles from St. Ignace. Father Claude Dablon, Father Marquette's superior at Quebec, wrote about Marquette's last day on earth. Father Dablon's words reveal Marquette's character and give an understanding of why Marquette's name and reputation were so great in his own day and still linger among the people of the northland where he traveled and taught:

> *The evening before his death, which was a Friday, he told them, very joyously, that it would take place on the morrow. He conversed with them during the whole day as to what would need to be done for his burial; about the manner in which they should inter him; of the spot that should be chosen for his grave; how his feet, his hands, and his face should be arranged; how they should erect a Cross over his grave. He even went so far as to counsel them, 3 hours before he expired, that as soon as he was dead they should take the little Hand-bell of his Chapel, and sound it while he was being put under-ground. He spoke of all these things with so great tranquility and presence of mind that one might have supposed that he was concerned with the death and*

*funeral of some other person, and not with his
own.*

Two years later a party of Ottawa Indians
whom Marquette had instructed visited his
grave. They exhumed the body and
prepared it according to tribal custom. They
then put the remains in a birchbark box
and set out for the mission at St. Ignace.
Nearly thirty canoes formed the funeral
procession, the Iroquois joining the
Algonquins, which lent more honor to the
ceremonial. The fact that the Ottawa
Indians let their traditional enemies, the
Iroquois, join them in order to pay tribute
to Father Marquette shows how much the
peace-making priest was revered. At St.
Ignace the Indians bearing Father
Marquette's remains were received with
solemn ceremony. The birchbark coffin was
buried in the chapel, which Marquette had
built, in a vault next to the altar where he
had officiated.

Father Marquette was one of the first
missionaries to bring Catholicism to
northern Michigan. For the next two
centuries Catholic priests endured the
hardships of the land, and to this day almost
all of the Indians in the area are Catholics.

Although none of Hemingway's family
was Catholic, the Indians he grew up with
were. Hemingway did not become a
Catholic until after he had been wounded
in Italy, and even then he was not a baptized
member of the faith. But Hemingway's

religious sympathies had their roots in the religion that Father Marquette first brought to the Indians of northern Michigan.

The Chippewas were allies of the French in their colonial wars with England, which broke out in 1744 after years of unrest. In the period, which elapsed between the defeat of the French in 1760 and the Treaty of Paris in 1763, much anti-British feeling was aroused among all of the Indians. The English were arrogant towards the Indians, gave them no presents, and tried instead to cheat them out of their scanty acquisitions. The French, meanwhile, inflamed the Indians and impressed them with the belief that the English were their deadly enemies. The Chippewas, filled with hatred for the English and naturally warlike fell in with the schemes of the Ottawa chief, Pontiac, and took the lead in the massacre at Fort Mackinac in 1763. The French, who were on good terms with the Chippewas, were unharmed. The Ottawas did not take part in the massacre.

Alexander Henry, one of the first English traders to go among the Indians, was at the Fort during the massacre, the bloodiest battle between Indians and white men in the history of northern Michigan. He lived to write about his experiences and described the difference between the two tribes and the location of their villages at the time of the massacre.

The Indians near Michilimackinac were

the Objibwas [sic] and Ottawas, the former of whom claimed the eastern section of Michigan, and the latter the western, their respective portions being separated by a line drawn southward from the Fort itself. The principal village of the Ojibwas contained about a hundred warriors, and stood on the island of Michilimackinac, now called Mackinac. There was another smaller village near the head of Thunder Bay. The Ottawas, to the number of two hundred and fifty warriors, lived at the settlement of L'Arbre Croche, on the shores of Lake Michigan, some distance southwest of the Fort. This place was then the seat of the old Jesuit mission of St. Ignace, originally placed by Father Marquette on the northern side of the Straits. Many of the Ottawa were nominal Catholics. They were all somewhat improved from their original savage condition, living in log houses, and cultivating corn and vegetables to such an extent as to supply the fort with provision, besides satisfying their own wants. The Ojibwas, on the other hand, were not in the least degree removed from their primitive barbarism.

Alexander Henry relates that the Ojibwas played a game of ball called "baggatiway" outside the gates of the Fort. About four hundred Indians were engaged in the game, while the inhabitants of the Fort, both soldiers and Canadians, numbered about ninety. The noise of the game diverted the officers and men and

permitted the Indians to take the Fort. The
English soldiers were strolling around
outside the Fort without weapons and did
not realize, until they heard the first shrill
war whoop, that the slaughter had begun in
the midst of the four hundred Indians
supposedly chasing the ball.

Henry had not gone to the game, but
instead was writing letters at his lodging
within the Fort. When he heard the war
whoop, he grabbed the only available gun,
a fowling piece filled with swan shot, and
ran to a window, too late to stop an Indian
from scalping an Englishman who was still
alive. He continued to watch the massacre
and noticed that the Canadians were not
attacked. The British trader immediately
left his lodging by the back door, climbed
over a fence, and went into the next-door
neighbor's house. The neighbor, a French-
Canadian named M. Langlade, was calmly
watching the slaughter with his family when
Henry begged him for refuge. Langlade
shrugged his shoulders and said, "*Que
voudriez-vous que j'en ferais?*" Luckily, a slave
of Langlade, a Pawnee woman, felt sorry for
Henry and led him to a room in the garret,
where she locked him in and took away the
key.

From his garret room Henry watched
the massacre:

> *Through an aperture, which afforded
> me a view of the area of the Fort, I beheld, in
> shapes the foulest and most terrible, the*

ferocious triumphs of barbarian conquerors.
The dead were scalped and mangled; the
dying were writhing and shrieking, under
the unsatiated knife and tomahawk; and
from the bodies of some, ripped open, their
butchers were drinking the blood, scooped up
in the hollow of joined hands, and quaffed
amid shouts of rage and victory. I was
shaken, not only with horror, but also with
fear. The sufferings, which I witnessed, I
seemed on the point of experiencing. No long
time elapsed before, every one being destroyed
who could be found, there was a general cry of
'All is finished.'

Henry was captured by the Ojibwas, but,
through a series of reprieves from death,
eventually was saved by the Ottawas. (The
Ottawas believed the Ojibwas had insulted
them by destroying the English at Fort
Mackinac without consulting the brother
tribe.) The Ojibwas were taking him and
other English prisoners in canoes to the
Isles of Castor (Beaver Island and the
islands surrounding it) when they were
tricked ashore by the Ottawas. The Ottawas
then took the Fort from the Ojibwas, and
soon Henry was safely on his way to
Montreal.

From the time of the massacre at Fort
Mackinac until the War of 1812, little of
historical import happened in the area of
Michigan Hemingway later wrote about.
Although Michigan had become a Territory
in 1805, the only inhabitants of this region

were the Ottawas and the missionaries who lived among them. During the American Revolution the post at Michilimackinac had been occupied by a British garrison. Although the Treaty of Paris of 1783 terminated the war and provided for Michilimackinac's surrender to the United States, British troops remained in control of the Fort until July 1796, following Jay's Treaty of 1794, which clearly established the Northwest Territory as an American possession. Later, during the War of 1812, the British, with the help of both the Ottawas and Chippewas, captured Mackinac Island again. Two years later the Americans attempted to retake the Fort, and many were slain. In the winter of 1814-15, when peace was concluded, the British evacuated the post, and the American troops took peaceable possession.

The Ottawas continued to live on the Lake Michigan shoreline from Mackinaw City to Harbor Springs until about 1840, when over half of the Indians moved to Canada because they feared being moved to Western reservations by the United States Government. Around 1827 the Catholics moved their mission from Seven Mile Point to Little Traverse, now Harbor Springs, and built a church of cedar logs. Not until 1853 were year-round, white residents living at Little Traverse. Before then the traders from Mackinac brought goods down to the Indians living near the mission. Several fishermen and a number of tradesmen formed the first permanent white population of Little Traverse.

In 1875-76 all the lands around Little Traverse Bay were thrown open to settlement. Soon farms were cleared in the forest. Real estate and professional men moved into offices in the new-framed buildings of Little Traverse. Docks were built, sawmills went up, and several newspapers were started. By 1880 the railroad connected the little town with Petoskey, and by 1881 Little Traverse was incorporated as the village of Harbor Springs. The village began growing as a resort center, beginning with the formation of the Harbor Point Association. Hemingway is his story "Ten Indians" described seeing the lights of Harbor Springs at night over Little Traverse Bay.

The city of Petoskey, the setting of Hemingway's novel, *The Torrents of Spring*, was named for a Chippewa Indian, Pe-to-se-ga. Pe-to-se-ga, which means "the Rising Sun," was given the first name of Ignatius by the Catholic missionaries when he was born in 1787. But when Ignatius Pe-to-se-ga became a chief, he decided to send his two oldest sons to a Protestant school in northern Ohio. The Catholic priests in the Little Traverse mission then excommunicated him, which precipitated many changes in his life. First he moved to the present location of Petoskey, and then his wife, who was a staunch Catholic, left him. Undaunted, Pe-to-se-ga took another wife, had fourteen children by her, worshipped in a nearby Protestant mission with his children, and lived to be ninety-four years old.

In 1873 a white man built the first house in Petoskey, and by 1875 the community had grown to 118 houses, ten stores, six saloons, three hotels, two churches, and a blacksmith shop. Petoskey became incorporated as a city in 1896 and became the seat of Emmet County in 1902 several years after the Hemingway family had started building their nearby summer home.

The wild, lumbering days in Michigan began about 1872, and by the turn of the century most of the pine forests were gone. Cadillac, which was mentioned in Hemingway's "The Light of the World," was typical of the lumbering boomtowns in northern Michigan. In 1872, Cadillac was a crude railroad station on the Grand Rapids & Indiana line in the midst of a dense pine forest stretching in all directions. Twenty years later Cadillac was a flourishing city of over 4,500 people, but the pine forests surrounding it were gone.

Many sections of northern Michigan, which Hemingway knew and wrote about, still seem to be a wilderness, with their second-growth forests, isolated lakes, and untouched streams. The flavor of the end of the nineteenth century is still intact in towns such as Harbor Springs and Horton Bay. The past lingers in this historically important area, which the first Europeans

discovered at about the same time the
Pilgrims reached Plymouth.

*   *   *

Footnote from *Along With Youth,*
Peter Griffen, Oxford University Press,
New York, Oxford, 1985, p.232.

The single most valuable work on
Hemingway's life in Michigan is Constance
Cappel Montgomery's *Hemingway in
Michigan* (New York, 1966). With scholastic
restraint and in a measured style,
Montgomery presents a "country," the
history of which includes prehistoric tribes,
Indian wars, and Christian martyrdom.
(Missionary Father Marquette requested he
be buried with his body arranged like the
corpses of Stone Age Indians in their
graves.) In legend the Windigo, a
cannibalistic man-beast, haunts the region.
In the silent autumn forest, you can almost
believe this is true.

*   *   *

From *Louise Erdrich:*
A Critical Companion,
Lorena L. Stookey, Greenwood Press,
Westport, Connecticut, 1999, p.22.

In Ojibwa tradition there are may
legends featuring the figure of the
"windigo," and in his book, *The Manitous,*

Ojibwa scholar Basil Johnston provides the following summary of accounts of this figure:

Weendigo (Weendigook or Weedigees): A giant cannibal (or cannibals). These manitous came into being in winter and stalked villagers and beset wanderers. Ever hungry, they craved human flesh, which is the substance that could sustain them. The irony is that having eaten human flesh, the Weendigoes grew in size, so their hunger and craving remained in proportion to their size; thus they were eternally starving. They could kill only the foolish and the improvident. (Johnston 247)

Chapter V

FOURTH OF JULY

Bitsy and Woody became more and more of a known couple at the Little Harbor Club. Both Mrs. Fay and Woody's mother, Mrs. Greer, were delighted. They had lunch together twice in one week at the club and had arranged several events where Woody would escort Bitsy. Woody felt like a puppet and was pulled along in the social swim.

He kept looking for that other girl. She never reappeared at the Pier Bar after the solstice. Woody knew that he would run into Trudy Mitchell when it was right, and if it was not right, they would not meet again. Woody was a fatalist and knew that events could not be altered or rushed. So he flew with Derek Haswell during the day and played Bitsy's games at night.

The gossip over lunch was the potential merging of the Woodward and Fay fortunes and how to curtail the encroaching beachhead of E.J. MacCloud. Everyone was shocked when he appeared at the second best table at the Saturday night dance several weeks ago. What they did not know was that MacCloud had hired Jose and Cliff and Joyce for the club from his winter base in Palm Springs. MacCloud had financed Jose's catering business and had sprung him from the Indian Wells Club where he would have died as the club manager. Jose was upward mobility himself and wanted his own sons, who were handsome, had American citizenship, and an American mother, to go to Yale like the sons of the members of the club did. MacCloud was helping him realize his dream both financially and socially. Cliff and Joyce worked for him and did everything he said.

Jose switched the seating late Saturday afternoon and rearranged the tables, so that they were helter skelter around the dance floor and not in the neat military fashion that they previously held. He worked with Mrs. Pierce and her committee, so that they thought it was their idea for the new table placement, flower arrangements, and more casual appearance of the main room. While the women concentrated on the tablecloth color and choice of flowers, Jose slipped in MacCloud and his table.

MacCloud had bribed his way into the club with paying for a new swimming pool, and now he had established a social beachhead challenging the Fays and the entire board of directors. He was beating them at their own game. He had an insider's role and was playing it for big stakes.

On the morning of the Fourth of July Woody arose with a hangover. As he took his morning shower and later ate his breakfast out on the harbor side screened-in porch, he made his plans for the day.

The Fourth of July was always his favorite holiday, and he liked the ones he had spent in Harbor Springs the best.

He put a little limejuice on the honeydew melon scooping it out, as he drank his thick, freshly ground roasted Mocha Java coffee. His Western omelet with the onions, tomatoes, and peppers fried into it and folded over just perfectly was his favorite leisurely breakfast. He usually just had Wheaties with fresh blueberries or strawberries in season. He always had freshly-squeezed orange juice, and Clara, the family cook, always liked to please Master Woody. She would take him on her wide lap when he was a little boy and have him help her shell peas, cut up strawberries, or anything else as an excuse to give the pale, thin boy some motherly love.

Woody loved the help and considered Clara and Joseph more family than some of his own aunts and uncles. They were the only ones, who as a child, had hugged him, wiped away his tears, or swatted him when he was bad. He grew up in the kitchen and never ate with his parents until he was seven. He spent more time with the kitchen help than he did with his own parents.

Woody thought that he would take the speedboat over to town around noon and just wander around in the crowds, which invaded Harbor Springs on the Fourth. The parade was at two in the afternoon. In the evening he always had dinner on the terrace of the club with his family and visiting relatives. When it was finally dark enough around 10:30 p.m., the fireworks were set off on a barge out in the harbor. He either watched from the club or took the speedboat out to the end of the Point where the fireworks burst overhead.

Woody loved the Fourth. Although he had lived in Europe and Asia, he was a real American. His strange, individualistic tastes and character were rooted in American history. His family fortune came from his entrepreneur grandfather who was an eccentric tinkerer of machines who also knew how to produce and sell his line of automobiles. Woody could fix any car, motorcycle, boat, or plane engine and had much of his grandfather's genius and verve. But he was living at a time without an American war, and his heroics were looked upon as thrill seeking by the bovine mentality, which was gripping the United States in the Fifties. If Woody had been born a generation earlier, he would have been looked upon as a war hero. As it was, he was just seen as a misfit or soldier of fortune.

The harbor was placid on the serene Fourth of July. A few boats gently plied back and forth. The Pointer, which was a wooden boat water taxi, left the Point dock for town carrying a few maids and chauffeurs who had the day off. They would be heading to the African-American nightclub with the good live music on the back roads of Harbor Springs. The water was the deep blue that only fresh lake water can attain. All of the artesian wells that bubbled out of the ground into the deep harbor gave Harbor Springs its present name replacing its Native American name. The trailing leaves of the large birch trees around the Woodward cottage gave a tasseled edging on a green canopy for Woody to look through as he read the down drafts on the bluff behind the town.

He jumped to his feet and propelled himself into motion. A jumpy and active person, Woody rarely was tired and had trouble finding activities to use up his demanding energy. He leapt down the stairs, ran

out the dock to the speedboat, unsecured it, and
leapt in. He roared across the harbor disturbing the
tranquility. He edged the boat into the covered
wooden boat shed on the opposite side and tied its
lines securely. His Chris Craft speedboat was made
of wood and was glazed to a mellow sheen. He had
the cushions covered with his trademark red instead
of the traditional nautical blue. Woody had to wait
for two months until they had just the right shade of
red for his Oldsmobile convertible and even now was
not entirely pleased with it.

Woody walked quickly up the center planks in
the darkened boat shed and burst out in the blazing
July sunlight. The crowds were already thick, and
the parade was over an hour away. Woody cut through
Zorn Park, past the public drinking fountain made
of beach stone, back of the Catholic Church, past
the Episcopal church where his mother went and
he used to go, down past the VFW Hall, and cut into
Main Street near Hovey's Drug Store. The Fay family
was sitting on the opposite corner with lawn chairs, a
cooler, and spread Hudson Bay blankets. On the
opposite side the MacClouds and their houseguests
plus a few of the waiters and waitresses from the Club
were encamped.

Woody ducked around the corner unnoticed and
headed for his favorite spot to watch the parade, a
no man's land at the end of Main Street where
everyone had to stand in the street, but you could
see the floats, the horses, the red, white, and blue
bestreamed antique and new Detroit cars, and the
marching bands which moved right towards you. This
was where many of the American Indians stood.

As Woody edged his way through the crowd, he
felt like he was in *Children of Paradise* or *Black Orpheus,*

two of his favorite films. Ahead of him crouching in the front row next to a group of rag tag Indian children, he saw her. The girl. The only one that he wanted to see in the crowds. The one who stood out from the throngs. He sidestepped around the edge of the crowd and dropped to his haunches in front of her. They looked at each other eye to eye, not talking. He sniffed the breeze. A slow smile began to play over her face.

"Again," he said.

"Again?" She answered.

They watched the parade. The noise, the confusion, the needs of Trudy's small charges kept them busy. She felt his tanned arm next to hers. He caught whiffs of her fresh, sweet smell between hot dogs and cigarette smoke. The sky was an eternal blue. The tar went soft on the road beneath their feet. Drops of perspiration collected on their upper lips and ran down their temples. And, when the last fire engine and the last float passed them, and Sister Elizabeth took her pupils back to the Mission School, they were alone, even though the crowds swirled around them, as they stood in the middle of the street.

"Let's go," Woody took her hand.

"Where?"

"With me."

He led her past the Catholic Church, the Little Harbor Club to the garage where he kept his car. He put down the top, dusted off her seat, helped her in, and they were off, out of town.

Woody headed north on the bluff along the shore, past the Harbor Point Golf Course, past Birchwood Farms, and up the hill where you could see as far as Northport Point to the south and to the west straddling the curve of the earth rode Beaver, Garden, High, and Whiskey Islands. They dipped down through a tunnel of dappled sunlight between the maple trees that created a psychedelic effect. Trudy did not know where they were going. She did not care. She put her head back on the black leather seat and watched the tree branches rush against the sky.

Woody quickly pulled off into the gravel turn-off high on the bluff overlooking the lake. They were alone. Everyone was in town. He led her to a little bower in the sumacs overlooking the brilliant sparkling of the forever reaching water.

"This is my favorite spot," he said.

"I like it."

"Here. Let me get a blanket from the car."

"No. Grass is okay." She stretched out her red, white, and blue printed skirt beneath her, as she sat down.

Woody laid beside her and pulled a piece of grass from its husk and chewed it. He could feel that tight ball inside of him relax. He did not need to be on alert. He rolled over on his back and just looked at the sky and sparkling water. They did not talk. They did not need to. They were in the safety of their den.

Finally Woody took a long piece of grass and tickled her bronze, rounded arm. She turned her liquid, trusting eyes on his clear, forever-seeing gray eyes. He pulled her to him, and they moved together pressing in hot earth coiled fashion. His arms clasped her breath away. Her legs wound around the back of his calves. He slowly opened her mouth with his tongue and fell into the cave. Her eyes held his. They almost forgot to breathe.

Several hours later when they lay side by side, holding hands, and looking at a single cloud in the sky, Woody thought that he had never been so happy in his entire life. Trudy was amazed that this Pointer stopped where she wanted him to stop, and they had only kissed for so long. She knew that he was aroused, but he did not argue or try to force himself on her. Her lips hurt from being nibbled on, and her earlobe stung where he bit her. Her legs rested over his in the warm sun.

"Sweetgrass. You're my little sweetgrass." He tickled her cheek with a piece of feathered grass.

She turned and looked him in the eyes. "Smoke," she said.

"Smoke? What do you mean smoke?"

"You smoke."

"You want me to smoke?" He began reaching for his Camels.

"No. You smoke." She put her hand on his hand, stopping him from reaching into the pocket of his khaki pants for the crushed pack of cigarettes. "No. You're like smoke. Smoke eyes. Smoke walk. Will o'wisp."

"That's good. We'll be 'Sweetgrass' and 'Smoke.' What a pair!"

They stood up, brushed themselves off, and got back into the convertible, but instead of heading back to Harbor and dinner at the Club, Woody decided to drive to his favorite bar in northern Michigan, Legs Inn. Legs Inn was located in the half American Indian town of Cross Village where he knew that Trudy would not be hassled. An eccentric Polish man, who fashioned a monument to himself out of beach stone with turrets and a fantasy exterior, built Legs Inn, but the inside was not less surrealistic with its tree trunks shaped and decorated like fantastical creatures. A strange Polish artistic heritage had melded into a glorification of a lost Polish past of castles, dragons, and knights, along with the nightmarish creation of frightening dream monsters. Trudy felt at home there, as did Woody.

At sunset everyone in the bar took their beers outside and watched the large knothole in the sky with the flames of Hell behind it slowly become extinguished in the molten liquid of the lake. Trudy and Woody had burgers and fries at their table in the corner. Woody tensed when a drunken American Indian man lurched towards their table.

"No. It's okay." Trudy put her hand on Woody's leg. "He's my uncle."

Billy Tabeshaw sat down at the pine table facing them. He did not say anything. They did not say anything. Finally Trudy spoke.

"How's fishing?" She asked.

"Okay."

"Lake trout?" Woody asked.

"Yep."

"Billy, this is Woody," said Trudy.

"Hi, Woody."

"Hello, Billy."

Two more Indians joined Billy.

"He calls me 'Sweetgrass'," said Trudy. Woody looked at her, shocked that she would share his private name for her.

"Good name," Billy answered.

Billy's face was lined from the hours on the big lake catching the large and plentiful lake trout. He was tough, and rumor had it, that he once walked barefoot from Harbor to Cross Village in winter. He had always liked Trudy and did not want her dragged down by some crazy white guy like her mother.

"Where you from?' He asked Woody.

"Detroit."

"No, here?"

"Point."

"Point?" Billy looked at the other two Indians.

"Yes."

"Too rich for my blood."

"Too rich for mine too," Woody answered. "Bunch of snobs."

"Bunch of snobs," Billy echoed.

Woody felt that he could always criticize his own kind. He would never judge others.

"You like Trudy?" Billy asked.

"I like Trudy." Woody put his hand solemnly on hers on the table. "I respect her. I would never hurt her."

"Okay Trudy?" Billy asked.

"Okay Billy."

"Okay." Billy and the other two Indians left their table.

Soon Woody and Trudy left.

"Well, I think I passed muster," Woody laughed, helping her into the car.

"You're okay."

They swooped down the back road going way over the legal driving limit. Woody put his car in the parking lot next to the railway station and led Trudy through the boathouse to his speedboat. Under cover of dusk they went across the calm darkening harbor to his favorite spot at the end of the Point. The lighthouse keeper and his family were out on the dock on the harbor side of the lighthouse.

Woody stalled the engines and pulled a woolen blanket out to cover them. He pulled Trudy next to him and covered her with his blanket tent.

"Two bugs in a rug," she said.

"Two bugs in a rug," he squeezed her feeling warm and happy.

Derek Haswell pulled his large family wooden boat near Woody's. The long Haswell boat was used as the yacht committee boat during NM races.

"Hey, Woody," Derek yelled across the water.

"Derek," Woody yelled back.

"Who you got with you?"

"Nobody," Woody whispered.

"Who?"

"Nobody," Woody said louder.

Trudy threw the blanket off and glared at him. "Not nobody."

Woody quickly pulled the blanket back up and covered her head. "Trudy," he answered to Derek.

Derek's boat slowly curved away in a half circle on the now black water. Voices floated back over the water.

"Whose he got in there?"

"Dunno."

"Want another beer?"

"Who was it?"

"Bitsy, I think," Derek said covering for his friend who had a dark-haired girl who was not part of their crowd on his boat.

Chapter E

From *Along With Youth*, Peter Griffin, pp. 32-33.

Then there were Nick Bolton and Billy Tabeshaw, two Indian sawyers. Bolton, who some of the local whites believed was a half-breed, lived with an Indian squaw named Annie and had two children, Eddy and Prudence. One night in town, Bolton drank whiskey with opium and, back at his shack, lay delirious half under the bed. Summoned by neighbor Joe Bacon, Clarence Hemingway had pumped Bolton's stomach out. But the next night Bolton went into Charlevoix, drank the same mixture, and died.

Most of all Ernest remembered the young Indian girls, some hardly into their teens, with whom he discovered the pleasures of adolescent sex. Years later he

created a composite of these experiences
in a short story and called the girl Trudy,
after Prudence, Nick Bolton's daughter.

*   *   *

In November of 1991, James Vol
Hartwell showed me Prudence Bolton's
unmarked grave behind the Greensky Hill
United Methodist Church between Horton
Bay and Charlevoix. On that same cold
November day, Jim Hartwell took me to
meet a former neighbor of the Richard
Bolton family, Jay Oliver. Jay was the
American Indian who had shown Hartwell
where Prudence Bolton was buried. Jay
Oliver was a well-traveled and intelligent
man who had entered the U.S. Army in
1942. He joined a medical unit stationed
in South Africa and the Persian Gulf. He
worked at a hospital in Iran for almost a year
before moving to Baghdad, Iraq, and then
to Jordan, Jerusalem, and Egypt. He
continued his medical career in civilian life
as clerk/technician in Charlevoix.

James Vol Hartwell is a resident of
Horton Bay and the owner of the Red Fox
Inn. His grandfather, Volli, hunted and
fished with Ernest Hemingway. Hemingway
also stayed at the Red Fox Inn when the
Dilworth's were full. Jim Hartwell is such a
fan of Hemingway's that he named his two
children, Ernest and Prudence.

Jay Oliver was an elderly man when I
interviewed him at his house in Charlevoix,

but he remembered the Hemingways, the Topasaches, the Boltons, and especially Prudence Bolton. He felt badly about Prudence's death and thought that she had been "led astray by Jim Castle," who was her partner in suicide. Oliver described Castle as "a criminal and a rough sort." He said that Prudence was three months pregnant when she died, presumably by Castle. He said that Prudence Bolton "was a girl of such incredible beauty that no man could resist her." But he also added "she was an easy mark because of her poverty."

Jay Oliver died in 1997 and is buried in the same cemetery as Prudence Bolton. His marked grave with a headstone is located in the circle of trees while Prudence's unmarked burial site is behind the new community center, which was built after 1991 when I first visited the old mission graveyard.

In an interview on July 24, 2000, I asked Jim Hartwell, if he thought that Ernest Hemingway had ever slept with Prudence Bolton. Most of the biographers deal with the sexual relationship as if it were a fantasy of Hemingway's. Jim Hartwell told me that Jay Oliver had told him that he overhead her sisters talking and said that Ernest "had tapped her."

Now Jay Oliver, Prudence Bolton, Jim Castle, and Ernest Hemingway are all dead, but stories and myths still are told and written about them. We will never know the truth, but this author believes that Prudence

Bolton initiated Ernest Hemingway in his first physical love experience. She was his first love and maybe the love of his life.

*   *   *

From "Three High School Stories," *Hemingway in Michigan,* pp. 40-45.

During his senior year, 1916-17, when most of the urge to write was being satisfied by his work for the school newspaper, Hemingway did find time to produce "Sepi Jingan," included in the November 1916 issue of the *Tabula.* Largely dialogue and with a Michigan background, this was a tale of violence and revenge told by an Ojibwa Indian.

Hemingway, in his previous high school writing for the newspaper, had used satire as well as straight reporting. In the case of "Judgment of Manitou," he had created a plot from either secondary sources or his imagination, but in "Sepi Jingan" he wrote about a setting he was familiar with, about an Indian he knew personally, and recounted a story which the Indian might have told him. In this more sophisticated story, Hemingway had the same clarity of narrative and certainty of style that he always had when he knew the subject from first-hand experience and had not created it out of his imagination.

＊　　＊　　＊

SEPI JINGAN
By Ernest Hemingway, '17

"'Velvets' like red hot pepper; 'P.A' like cornsilk. Give me a package of 'Peerless.'"

Billy Tabeshaw, long, lean, copper-colored, hamfaced and Ojibway, spun a Canadian quarter onto the counter of the little northwoods country store and stood waiting for the clerk to get his change from the till under the notion counter.

"Hey, you robber!" Yelled the clerk. "Come back here!"

We all had a glimpse of a big, wolfish-looking, husky dog vanishing through the door with a string of frankfurter sausages bobbing, snake-like, behind him.

"Darn that blasted cur! Them sausages are on you, Bill."

"Don't cuss the dog. I'll stand for the meat. What's it set me back?"

"Just twenty-nine cents, Bill. There was three pounds of 'em at ten cents, but I et one of 'em myself."

Bill's dusky face cracked across in a white-toothed grin. He put his package of tobacco under his arm and slouched out of the store. At the door he crooked a finger at me and I followed him out into the cool twilight of the summer evening. At the far end of the wide porch three pipes glowed in the dusk.

"Ish," said Bill, "they're smoking 'Stag!'

It smells like dried apricots. Me for 'Peerless.'"

Bill is not the redskin of the popular magazine. He never says "ugh." I have yet to hear him grunt or speak of the Great White Father at Washington. His chief interests are the various brands of tobacco and his big dog, "Sepi Jingan."

We strolled off down the road. A little way ahead, through the gathering darkness, we could see a blurred figure. A whiff of smoke reached Bill's nostrils. "God, that guy is smoking 'Giant'! No, it's 'Honest Scrap'! Just like burnt rubber hose. Me for 'Peerless.'"

The edge of the full moon showed above the hill to the east. To our right was a grassy bank. "Let's sit down," Bill said. "Did I ever tell you about Sepi Jingan?"

"Like to hear it," I replied.

"You remember Paul Black Bird?"

"The new fellow who got drunk last Fourth of July and went to sleep on the Pere Marquette tracks?"

"Yes. He was a bad Indian. Up on the Upper Peninsula he couldn't get drunk. He used to drink all day—everything. But he couldn't get drunk. Then he would go crazy; but he wasn't drunk. He was crazy because he couldn't get drunk.

"Paul was Jack-fishing (spearing fish illegally) over on Witch Lake up on the upper, and John Brandar, who was game warden, went over to pinch him. John always did a job like that alone: so next day, when he didn't show up, his wife sent me over to look for him. I found him, all right. He was lying at the end of the portage, all spread out, face down, and a pike-pole stuck through his back.

"They raised a big fuss and the sheriff hunted all over for Paul; but there never was a white man yet could catch an Indian in the Indian's own country.

"But with me, it was quite different. You see, John Brandar was my cousin.

"I took Sepi, who was just a pup then, and we trailed him (that was two years ago). We trailed him to the Soo, lost the trail, picked it up at Garden River, in Ontario; followed him along the north shore to Michipicoten; and then he went up to Missainabie and 'way up to Moose Factory. We were always just behind him, but we never could catch up. He doubled back by the Abittibi and finally thought he'd ditched us. He came down to this country from Mackinaw.

"We trailed him, though, but lost the scent and just happened to hit this place. We didn't know he was here, but he had us spotted.

"Last Fourth of July I was walking by the P.M tracks with Sepi when something hit me alongside the head and everything went black.

"When I came to, there was Paul Black Bird standing over me with a pike-pole and grinning at me!

"'Well,' he smiled, 'you have caught up with me; ain't you glad to see me?'

"There was when he made a mistake. He should have killed me then and everything would have been all right for him. He would have, if he had been either drunk or sober, but he had been drinking and was crazy. That was what saved me.

"He kept prodding me with the pike-pole and kidding me. 'Where's your dog, dog man? You and he have followed me. I will kill you both and then slide you onto the rails.'

"All the time I kept wondering where Sepi was. Finally I saw him. He was crawling with his belly on the earth toward Black Bird. Nearer and nearer he crawled and I prayed that Paul wouldn't see him.

"Paul sat there, cussing and pricking me with the long pike-pole. Sepi crawled closer and closer. I watched him out of the tail of my eye while I looked at Paul.

"Suddenly Sepi sprang like a shaggy thunderbolt. With a side snap of his head, his long, wolf jaws caught the throat.

"It was really a very neat job, considering. The Pere Marquette Resort Limited removed all the traces. So, you see, when Marquette tracks you weren't quite right. That Indian couldn't get drunk. He only got crazy on drink.

"That's why you and me are sittin' here, lookin' at the moon, and my debts are paid and I let Sepi steal sausages at Hauley's store.

"Funny, ain't it?

"You take my advice and stay of that 'Tuxedo'—'Peerless' is the only tobacco.

"Come on, Sepi."

*   *   *

"Sepi Jingan," is the most mature of Hemingway's high school stories. In it the young writer drew directly from the Michigan countryside and people he knew. "Hauley's store" is probably the false-front country store in the town of Horton Bay. "Billy Tabeshaw" appears again as a fictional character in the stories "The Doctor and the Doctor's Wife" and "Ten Indians." But Billy Tabeshaw was also the name of a flesh-and-blood Indian who lived in the Indian camp near the Hemingway cottage. Hemingway describes Billy Tabeshaw as being long and lean in "Sepi Jingan." However, he later described him in "The Doctor and the Doctor's Wife" as being fat, not long and lean.

Although the story, which Billy tells the summer resident in "Sepi Jingan" may have been fictional (a fictional story within a fictional story), the possibility exists that it actually could have happened. The real Billy Tabeshaw could have tracked an Indian named Paul Black Bird for two years, and his dog, Sepi Jingan, might have killed a man.

Hemingway himself probably did not know an Indian by the name of Paul Black Bird, but he might have fictionalized an Indian he did know and used the historic Indian name of "Blackbird," the name of the famous Ottawa chief for whom the museum in Harbor Springs was named.

An elderly neighbor of the Hemingways remembered several Indians, whom he had known personally and whom Ernest probably also had known, who had met death when they had fallen asleep on the railroad tracks. The tracks of the Pere Marquette railroad ran parallel to the side of Walloon Lake where the Hemingway cottage stands. This same neighbor said that the father of Tommy Mitchell, an Indian who was a friend of Ernest's and who was fictionalized in "The Light of the World," lived in Petoskey. One night Tommy Mitchell's father was drunk; he fell asleep on the railroad tracks and was killed instantly when run over by a train. Another Indian family from near Walloon Lake, the Quazicums, had four boys, and of these four only one was not run over by a train while drunk. Hemingway undoubtedly heard about these Indians and maybe even knew them when he was a boy.

The reference in "Sepi Jingan" to the Upper Peninsula means the upper part of Michigan, which is beyond the Straits of Mackinac. This allusion plus the one about the Pere Marquette tracks definitely sets the scene of this story near the Hemingway summer home on Walloon Lake.

*   *   *

Of these three stories, "Sepi Jingan"
seems to foreshadow Hemingway's later
work most accurately. The humor in "Sepi
Jingan" comes from the more subtle
contrasts of the Indian's character while
in "A Matter of Colour" the sophomoric
humor is still broad and like his later
newspaper writing for the Toronto *Star
Weekly*. The involved plot and surprise
ending of "Judgment of Manitou"
foreshadow such later stories as "The
Snows of Kilimanjaro," while the hidden
recesses of character and the theme that
people are not what they seem to be link
"Sepi Jingan" with such later stories as
"The Sea Change" and "The Short Happy
Life of Francis Macomber."

Not one to be attracted by the easy
sentimentalism of the writing in 1916-17,
Hemingway had already chosen his subject
matter of rough men pitted against nature
and their own characters, of murderers—
Indian, in this case—explaining life's rules
to the young initiate, and of the life in and
about the prize ring. He would later expand
these themes but not change his basic thesis.

In these three high school stories
Hemingway first exhibited his concern with
death, often violent death. He even used
the clipped dialogue, the fast-paced action,
and the diamond-hard brilliance of style
which became his trademarks. Although
Hemingway wrote these stories when he was

only seventeen and eighteen, they all bear
his unmistakable stamp.

*   *   *

In a short story called "Billy Gilbert"
written by Ernest Hemingway and included
in *Along with Youth* by Peter Griffin, the
character is another version of Billy Tabashaw
or Tapasach, which is the correct spelling. In
this story Billy is an Ojibway who lived near
Susan Lake and who has two children named
Beulah and Prudence. Billy was a good farmer
and in the story Hemingway had Billy go to
the Soo and enlist in the Black Watch. When
Billy came home with medals and ribbons for
his bravery, the people in Horton Bay made
fun of his kilts. Being made fun of as an Indian
wearing skirts was not the kind of
homecoming Billy had pictured.

He hiked up the road to Susan Lake
and found his shack deserted and
padlocked. He found out that his wife had
run off with Simon Green's son. Again
Hemingway used the real name of one of
the most respected Native Americans in the
area. Simon Green died of old age within a
month of Prudence Bolton's suicide and is
listed in the same record book. In the story
Hemingway has Billy whistle: "It's a long way
to Tipperary, It's a long way to go."

So again Ernest Hemingway uses
Prudence, Billy, and other Indian
neighbors as fictional characters in his
writing.

Chapter VI

HARBOR SPRINGS

Trudy knew that she had to have a job. Her garden was growing beans, big beets, and lettuce, but there wasn't enough food for the table. Dick Mitchell was laid off from the painting job at the boat yard where he thought that he would be all summer. Her mother needed medicine. Sister Elizabeth only used her on the Fourth.

She decided to walk up the bluff and consult Alice Mitchell about what to do. Aunt Alice was resourceful and always helped Trudy make the correct choice.

The day was hot, and no one was out in the streets in the morning sun. Trudy was dripping by the time she had climbed the bluff. Her Aunt Alice was sitting on the porch by herself waiting for her when she rounded the corner. Trudy had called earlier, and Alice had detected a quaver in Trudy's voice that lead her to block out two hours exclusively for Trudy.

"Hot enough for you," Alice called to Trudy, as she came up the walk.

"Sure is."

"Gonna be a scorcher. How's about some lemonade?"

"Sounds good to me."

When they were settled down in the large wicker rocking chairs facing the lake, Alice started to try to get at the source of the quaver in Trudy's voice.

"So you're looking for a job?"

"Uh-huh."

"Any luck?"

"No."

"No babysitting jobs?"

"I'm too old for that."

"You're never too old for that. Only two jobs that prepare you for marriage are babysitting and housecleaning."

"I don't want to."

"Well, young lady, you're in for a set back, because that is what most women here do in the summer."

"I know."

"What about the five and dime?"

"No."

"Why not?"

"Just not."

"That would be a perfect job. You could learn retailing and keep an eye on Johnnie at the same time."

"No."

"That Johnnie is a good catch. If you don't snap him up, some other girl will."

"That's okay."

"What do you mean? You two have a fight?" Alice was concerned that if Trudy did not marry Johnnie in the year after her high school graduation that she would never have another chance, or worse yet fall into a situation like her mother did.

"No. No fight."

"What then?"

"He's boring."

"Boring. Johnnie Moore boring? What has that got to do with it? He's from a good Christian family. He's a nice looking boy and a hard worker. He'd be a good family man like his father. Boring! You sound like one of those girls from the Point."

Trudy stared at the water.

"So do you have something better in mind?" asked Alice, knowing she would stump Trudy on that one.

"Woody Woodward," Trudy whispered.

"Woody Woodward? What do you mean?"

"Woody Woodward from the Point."

"Oh, my god," Alice leaned back in her chair and fanned herself. "You're not tangled up with *him?*"

"I see him."

"You *see* him? How often do you *see* him?"

"All the time."

"My heavens," Alice was counting nine months ahead. "Where did you meet him?"

"Pier Bar," said Trudy, not telling her aunt that Alice was responsible for having her take the dress box for Mrs. Fay.

"You know he's wild. I knew his father. Would take up cuffs for him. His mother will never allow this." She was thinking aloud. "You must stop seeing him, before . . ."

"Before what?"

"Before, I hate to say this to you, Trudy, dear, but at your age, and with your mother and everything . . ."

"Before what?"

"Before you get in a family way," Alice blurted it out and reached over to touch Trudy's shoulder.

"Impossible." Trudy rocked hard.

"Nothing is impossible, dear."

"Not 'immaculate conception'," Trudy smiled.

"What are you talking about? Are you going to Mass again?"

"No. I don't have sex with Woody," Trudy blurted out to her dumbfounded aunt.

Alice had no response then or later. She talked about the weather, her clients, village gossip, but she never returned to the subject of Woody and Trudy and their sex life, or lack of it. Finally Trudy knew that she would not find the answers to her questions at her Aunt Alice's house and decided to descend into the village. The church bells pealed at noon, and the siren in the center of town made her look at her watch to check the time.

A few tourists dragged from store to store and ate ice cream cones under the shop awnings. The large ship the "North American" was moored at the city dock for three hours while the tourists browsed at Harbor Springs on their cruise of the Great Lakes. Trudy thought of going to Irwin's drug store where the Nancy Drew books were sold, but decided that she needed to wear a skirt to ask for a job there. The five and dime was next door, and she walked by it. The next shop was Haynes Photography, but they always had their summer help hired by May.

Alex Du Bois who had his winter shop on the Riviera owned the next store. He had small Picassos

and Miros on Oriental rugs in the window. Trudy
went into the European gloom of the shop, but Mr.
Du Bois was out. His nephew told her that they did
not need help.

The shop after the Du Bois shop changed hands
every summer. This summer they specialized in wind
chimes, which tinkled over the bric-a-brac littering
the counters. They did not need help.

The next store belonged to Mrs. Rosenbloom,
and a big sign "Rosenbloom's" hung out over the
sidewalk. Even though the resorters were anti-
Semitic, they all brought their children to Mrs.
Rosenbloom's shop for new summer sailor caps,
Janzten bathing suits, and Harbor Springs T-shirts.

"Hello, Trudy," called Mrs. Rosenbloom from her
stool in the back of the store. She was the ultimate
saleswoman and never missed a sale whether it is large
or small. She let Trudy go through all of the piles of
underwear and shorts before she approached her.

"Can I help you?"

"No, not really," said Trudy, because she saw some
real customers enter the store and did not want to
lose a sale for Mrs. Rosenbloom.

Trudy watched her as she trailed the family
around the store; sending the girl to try on a swimsuit
and helping the boy select a beach towel. When the
parents and children left the store, they carried two
big paper bags crammed with summer clothes and
accessories. The customers were happy that they had
bought so much for so much less than they would
have paid in Chicago, and Mrs. Rosenbloom was
delighted that she had sold some outfits that had
been on her shelves for ten years. All of the summer
people, who owned cottages in the nearby area,
would come in and paw through Mrs. Rosenbloom's

merchandise, some of which they had remembered seeing right after World War II.

"So, Trudy, can I help you now?"

"Mrs. Rosenbloom, I'm looking for a job."

"Oh, dear. I hired one high school girl, but I can't afford another. I'm in here every day."

"Well, I thought I'd try . . ." Trudy turned to leave.

"What about over at the Indian Gift Shop across the street. I heard they lost some help last week."

"Okay. Thanks, Mrs. Rosenbloom."

Trudy crossed Main Street to the little shop leaning against the brick mass of the Lyric Theater. Don Assawgon owned the Indian Gift Shop, and was the chief of the remaining Ottawa tribe. He was a tall, affable man, who had graduated from the University of Michigan, and was liked by Native Americans, summer people, and the year around people of Harbor Springs. Every year he was a write-in candidate for mayor, but he always declined.

Don was sorting quill boxes when Trudy entered.

"Little Trudy, all grown up," he smiled.

"Hi, Don."

"I've been meaning to talk to you. I put your name down for Indian Princess for the Pow-Wow in August."

"How many running?"

"There's three running this year, but you're the prettiest by far."

"Sure, Don." Trudy smirked. "By the way, Mrs. Rosenbloom said you might need some help in the store?"

"Sure do. Lost two people last weeks. Know how to use a cash register?"

"No, but I'll learn."

"How about coming in tomorrow morning around nine? We open at ten."

"Sounds good. Thanks, Don."

"You're helping me. Tell your mother I can use some more quill baskets."

*   *   *

Trudy loved working at the store for Don Assawgon. He was the perfect boss, more of a mentor than a boss, who took Trudy under his protection. Trudy liked talking to the tourists about her Native American background and the town of Harbor Springs. She was getting a reputation of being a historian, and customers came back just to talk to her. She used her own application of Mrs. Rosenbloom's sales techniques, and Don was pleased to notice that the sales figures had increased by twenty per cent, since Trudy had been there.

Trudy was able to stop at Wagner's Market on the way home and buy nourishing food for her family. With the blood pressure medicine that she bought at Hovey's, there was not much left over for the new pair of shoes she needed. But Trudy was happy and contented with her life at the moment.

"Trudy, do you think we should put out more quill boxes?" asked Don.

"Maybe. But just a few with the balsam-scented bags that the children can touch and smell might be better. Less wear and tear."

"You are right," he said putting the beautiful quill boxes on a shelf behind the counter where they could be seen and had to be asked for.

"Are you ready for a fitting for your Indian Princess costume? You know the Pow-Wow is on August eighth."

"I can have my aunt Alice fit it for me. She is the

best seamstress in town."

"Of course, of course. But can she work with deer skin?"

"She can work with anything."

At that moment Woody came into the store, and Trudy asked Don for a break. They went to Anderson's soda fountain for a cherry Coke and a slice of homemade cherry pie. Woody never took Trudy anywhere with his friends from the club. Instead they went to movies in Petoskey and bars in Boyne City or to Legs Inn. She knew it was because she was a local, and a half-breed to boot. So his asking her to Anderson's was a surprise to her. In broad daylight. In Harbor Springs.

"Best cherry Coke in the world," he slurped.

"Right."

"How would you know? You've never traveled outside of Harbor Springs."

"I just know," answered Trudy confidently.

"That's what I like about you, Trudy. You are *so* polite, but you don't let me get on my high horse."

"High horse?"

"Yes, my damn high horse."

"I'd like to see 'Smoke' on a highest of all horses," she smiled.

"By the way, I have a present for you on your birthday."

"My birthday?"

"Don told me that it was the week before the Pow-Wow, August 1st?"

"Uh-huh."

"I'll pick you up at the store then. Tomorrow night?"

"Uh-huh."

"Gotta run," he paid the bill and literally ran out

of Anderson's.

Trudy looked at herself in the mirror opposite the soda fountain. She still saw "Smoke" where he had sat next to her a minute before. Every time he appeared, it was a miracle. When he left, she could still see his wispy outline. He lived with her now in her head and was as close to her as her own shadow.

Chapter F

From the *History of the Ottawa and Chippewa Indians of Michigan,* pp.64-71.

Becoming Protestant—Persecutions—Second Attempt to go to School—Trials With Indian Agent—Governor Lewis Cass— Struggles During Education—Getting Married— Coming Home—Government Interpreter and Postmaster.

The next five years passed among my people, doing a little of everything, laboring, teaching, and interpreting sermons among the Protestant missions—for there were by this time two Protestant missions established among the Ottawas of Arbor Croche, one at Bear River, now Petoskey, and another at Middle Village or Arbor Croche proper, where I acted as an assistant teacher and interpreter. I met much opposition from the Catholic community, because I had already become a Protestant and left the Romish Church, not by any personal persuasion, however, but by terrible conviction on reading the word of God— "That there is no mediator between God and man but one which is Christ Jesus, who was crucified for the remission of sins." One Sunday, some friend persuaded me to come to the church, but when the priest saw me he came and forcibly ejected me out of the room. The same priest left the Indian country soon afterwards, and it seems he went to England, and just before he died he wrote to my sister a very touching epistle, in which he said nothing about himself or any one in Little Traverse, but from the beginning to the end of the letter he expressed himself full of sorrow for what he had done to me when in this country among the Indians, and asking of me forgiveness for his wrongs towards me.

Soon after the council of Detroit, I became very discontented, for I felt that I ought to have gone through with my medical studies, or go to some college and receive a degree and then go and study some profession. But where is the means to take me through for completing my education? Was the question every day. So, after one payment of the treaty of 1855, late in the fall of 1856, I went up to Mr. Gilbert, who was then Indian agent, and made known to him my intention, and asked him if he would aid me towards completing my education, by arranging for me to receive

the benefit of our educational fund, which
was set apart at the last council for the
education of the Indians in this State. But
he would not. He bluffed me off by saying
he was sorry I had voted the "black
republican ticket," at the general election,
which took place that fall of 1856. This was
the first time that the Indians ever voted on
general election. Mr. Gilbert was at North
Port, Grand Traverse, on Election Day,
managing the Indian votes there, and he
sent a young man to Little Traverse to
manage the voting there and sit as one of
the Board at the Little Traverse election.
He sent the message to Indians to vote no
other ticket but the democratic ticket. At
this election there were only two republican
votes in Little Traverse, one of which was
cast by myself. As I was depositing my ballot,
this young man was so furiously enraged at
me he fairly gnashed his teeth, at which I
was very much surprised, and from my
companion they tried to take away the ticket.
Then they tried to make him exchange his
ticket, but he refused. We went out quickly,
as we did not wish to stay in this excitement.
At that time I felt almost sorry for my people,
the Indians, forever being citizens of the
State, as I thought they were much happier
without these elections.

          After payment of our annuities, as the
vessel was about starting off to take the
Indian agent to Mackinac, they had already
hoisted the sails, although there was not
much wind, and I thought, this was the last

chance to get to Mackinac. As I looked toward the vessel I wept, for I felt terribly downcast. As they were going very slowly toward the harbor point, I asked one of the Indian youngsters to take me and my trunk in a canoe to the vessel out there. I had now determined to go, in defiance of every opposition, to seek my education. I hurried to our house with the boy, to get my trunk and bid good bye to my aged father, and told him I was going again to some school outside, and if God permitted I hoped to return again to Little Traverse. All my father said was, "Well, my son, if you think it is best, go." And away we went. We overtook the vessel somewhere opposite Little Portage, and as I came aboard the agent's face turned red. He said, "Are you going?" I said, "Yes sir, I am going." So nothing more was said. The greater part of the night was spent by the agent and the captain gambling with cards, by which the agent lost considerable money. We arrived the next day at Mackinac, and again I approached the Indian agent with request if he could possibly arrange for me to have the benefit of our Indian educational fund, set apart for that purpose at the council of Detroit 1855; and again he brought up the subject of my voting. Then I was beginning to feel out of humor, and I spoke rather abruptly to him, saying, "Well, sir, I now see clearly that you don't care about doing anything for my welfare because I voted for the republican party. But politics have nothing to do with my education; for the Government of the United States owes us that amount of money, not politics. I was one of the councilors when that treaty was made, and I will see some other men about this matter, sir." His face turned all purple, and as I was turning about to keep away from him, he called me back, saying, "Mr. Blackbird, how far do you intend to go to get your education?" I said, "I intend to go to Ann Arbor University, sir." "Well, I will do this much for you: I will pay your fare to Detroit. I am going by way of Chicago, but you can go down by the next boat, which will be here soon from Chicago." I thanked him, and he handed me money enough to pay my fare to Detroit.

So I reached Detroit, and went to Dr. Stuben's house and inquired my way to Governor Cass' residence; and when I knocked at the door, behold it was he himself came to the door. I shook hands with him and said, "My friend, I would like to speak to you a few moments." "Is it for business?" He asked. "Yes sir, it is." "Well, my boy, I will listen to what you have to say." I therefore began, saying, "Well, my friend, I come from Arbor Croche. I am the nephew of your old friend, "Warrior Wing," am seeking for education, but I have no means, and I come to see you expressly to acquaint you with my object, and to ask you the favor of interceding for me to the Government to see if they could possibly do something towards defraying my expenses in this object. That is all I have to say." The old man raised his spectacles and said, "Why, why! Your object is a very good one. I was well acquainted with your uncle in the frontier of Michigan during the war of 1812. Have you seen and told the Indian agent of this matter?" "Yes sir, I have asked him twice, but he would not do anything for me." "Why, why! It seems to me there is ample provision for your people for that object, and has been for the last twenty years. What is the matter with him?" I said, "I don't know, sir." "Well, well; I am going to Washington in a few days, and shall see the Indian Commissioner about this matter, and will write to you from there on the subject. I know they can do something toward defraying your expenses. Where do you intend to go?" I said, "I don't know, yet, sir, but I thought of going to the University at Ann Arbor." "Is it possible? Are you prepared to enter such a college?" I told him I thought I was. "Well, sir, I think you had better go to Ypsilanti State Normal School instead of Ann Arbor: it is one of the best colleges in the State." This was the first time I ever heard of that school, and it sounded quite big to me; so I told him that I would gladly attend that school, provided I had means to do so. "Well, then, it is settled. You shall go to Ypsilanti, and I will direct my letter to Ypsilanti when I write to you; and now mind nobody, but just go about your business." After thanking him for his good counsel I shook hands with the old man and left.

The next day was a terrible snow storm,

but, however, I started out for Ypsilanti,
which is only about thirty miles from Detroit.
Of course, as I was totally a stranger in the
place, I put up at a hotel, although my
means were getting very short. The next day
I went about to find out all about the
institution, cost of tuition, and private board,
etc., and saw some of the professors of the
institution, but I did not dare to make any
arrangements for a steady boarding place
and begin school for fear Governor Cass
should fail of getting help from the
Government. Therefore, instead of
beginning to go to school, I went and hired
out on a farm about three miles from the
city, and continued to work there for about
three weeks before I heard from Governor
Cass. At last the old farmer brought a
package of letters from the post office, one
of which was post marked at Washington
D.C., and another from Detroit. I fairly
trembled as I opened the one which I
thought was from Governor Cass, as between
doubt and hope, but my fears were suddenly
changed into gladness, and quickly as
possible I settled with the farmer, and away
I went towards the city, singing as I went
along. By intercession of Governor Cass, it
was proposed to pay my whole expenses—
board, clothes, books, tuition, etc. The other
letter was from the Indian agent, calling me
to come down to Detroit, as he had already
received some instructions from the
Commissioner of Indian Affairs to look after
me and to arrange the matters of my

schooling at Ypsilanti State Normal School. O, how I did hate to have to meet the Indian Agent again on this subject; to stand before him, and to have him think that I had overcome him, and succeeded in spite of his opposition to my desire. O, how I wished this matter could have been arranged without his assistance. However, I started out for Detroit the same evening I received these communications, and went to the agent. He never even said, "How do you do?" But immediately began, saying "Well, sir, how much do you think that it will cost for your schooling at Ypsilanti?" "I don't know, sir," I responded. "Well, who knows? I think you ought to know, as you have been there," he said, in a gruff voice. "I have not been to school at all, sir," I said, "but have been working on a farm up to this morning." "Working on a farm, eh? I thought you came here on purpose to attend school?" "I did, sir, but you know I was very short of means, so I had to do something to keep me alive." "Can't you tell me the cost for your board per week?" "The private board is from $3.50 to $4 per week, sir, as according to accommodation." "How much for books and clothing?" "I don't know, sir; but I think I have enough clothing for at least one year."

In the morning I went back to Ypsilanti, and with the aid of the professors of the institution I got a good boarding place. I attended this institution almost two years and a half, when I could not hold out any longer, as my allowance for support from

the Government was so scanty it did not pay
for all my necessary expenses. I have always
attributed this small allowance to the Indian
Agent who was so much against me. I tried
to board myself and to live on bread and
water; and therefore hired a room which
cost me 75 cents a week, and bought bread
from the bakeries, which cost me about 50
cents a week, and once in awhile I had fire-
wood as I did not keep much fire. I stood it
pretty well for three months, but I could
not stand it any longer. I was very much
reduced in flesh, and on the least exertion
I would be trembling, and I began to be
discouraged in the prosecution of my
studies. By this time I was in the D class, but
class F was the graduating class in that
institution, which I was exceedingly anxious
to attain; but I imagined that I was beginning
to be sick on account of so much privation,
or that I would starve to death before I could
be graduated, and therefore I was forced to
abandon my studies and leave the
institution.

As I did not have any money to pay my
passage homeward, I went about working
and occasionally lecturing on the subject of
the Indians of Michigan, and at last I had
enough means to return home and try to
live once more according to the means and
strength of my education. September 4th,
1858, I was joined in wedlock to the young
lady who is still my beloved wife, and now
we have four active children for whom I ever
feel much anxiety that they might be

educated and brought up in a Christian manner. Soon after I came to my country my father died at a great age. The first year we lived in Little Traverse we struggled quite hard to get along, but in another year I was appointed U.S. Interpreter by the Hon. D.C. Leach, U.S. Indian Agent for Mackinac Indian Agency, to whom I ever feel largely indebted, and I continued to hold this situation under several of his successors in office.

During the Rebellion I was loyal to the Government, and opposed the bad white men who were then living in the Indian country, who tried to mislead my people as to the question of the war, to cause them to be disloyal. After the war was over, I was appointed as an auxiliary prosecutor of the Indian soldier claims, as quite a number of our people also helped to put down this rebellion, and many were killed and wounded. But most of this kind of business I performed without reward.

Before I was fairly out as Interpreter, I was appointed with a very small salary as postmaster at Little Traverse, now Harbor Springs, where I discharged my duties faithfully and honestly for eleven years. But the ingress of the white population in this Indian country increased much from 1872-73 and onward. The office was beginning to be a paying one, and I was beginning to think that I was getting over the bridge, when others wanted the office, my opponents being the most prominent persons. Petitions were forwarded to Washington to have me removed, although no one ever had any occasion to complain of having lost his money or letter through this office during my administration. At last, the third assistant postmaster general at Washington wrote me a kind of private letter, stating that the main ground of the complaint was, that my office was too small and inconvenient for the public, and advising me to try and please the public as well as I could. And consequently I took what little money I had saved and built a comfortable office, but before the building was thoroughly completed I was removed. This left me penniless in this cold world, to battle on and to struggle for my existence; and from that time hence I have not held any office, nor do I care to. I only wish I could do a little more for the welfare of my fellow-beings before I depart for another world, as I am now nearly seventy years old, and will soon pass away. I wish my readers to remember that the above history of my existence is only a short outline. If time and means permitted, many more interesting things might be related.

Chapter VII

LITTLE HARBOR CLUB

In the nineteen Fifties the Little Harbor Club was a rich teenager's paradise. The wealthy parents decided that since they knew their children would be drinking anyway, they would give them the free reign of the club and not observe the legal drinking age. This way the teenagers would not be going into town to the bars or drinking and driving. The entire resort community was shocked the summer before when a car full of teenagers from the Point and Weque ran off the road and into a large pine above Forest Beach killing two girls and one boy, but leaving the drunken teenage male driver unharmed. The parents decided to relax the rules and keep their children in a place where they could walk home.

The babysitters were Cliff, Joyce, and Jose, and as such, they monitored, but did not judge the behavior of their young charges. The parents would leave the club before midnight, but the downstairs bar would stay open for as long as there were drinkers. But instead of moderating their behavior as the parents thought would happen, the heavy drinking and arrogant behavior of the group knew no limits. In the years of "La Dolce Vita" this subculture of the offspring of the wealthy American Midwest knew few bounds. When *Fortune* magazine ran a photo story on Harbor Point, the reporter noted in a caption under several of the younger set that they were "extremely self-assured." Most of the younger group had assumed the elite and insular views of their parents which they annexed onto the cruel, territorial, and exclusive behavior of teenage gangs. "West Side Story" made sense to the young adults at the Little Harbor Club.

Woody's mother and Bitsy's mother both wanted to make sure that their children would not be casualties of the hedonistic lifestyle which they daily observed at the Little Harbor Club. They both knew that a pairing between their children was risky, but at least was within the inner circle of their world.

Bunny Fay knew that Bitsy was already "old hat" and had burnt her bridges in the East. In a way that is what allowed Mrs. Fay to entertain the thought of a union with Ernest Woodward, Junior's wild son, Woody. He was far too worldly and experienced for her taste, and heaven only knows what he learned in his years in Europe and Indochina. She preferred a marriage when the groom was straight out of Princeton or Yale, with maybe one brief trip to Paris during a college summer to broaden his views.

Woody, on the other hand, had been on his own and living abroad for six years now. She felt his behavior was a little too risk-taking, and some of his antics in the plane bordered on suicidal. She had forbade Bitsy to fly with him anymore, since the afternoon she observed him flying across the harbor close to the water below the masts of the moored sailboats.

But on the other hand, she had known him his whole life and knew both of his parents. She thought that his father had been a mild-mannered eccentric, and his mother wore the pants in the family. With Lucretia Greer to help keep Woody in line, she might manage.

Mrs. Fay and Mrs. Greer had made reservations for lunch at the club that very day. Jose had the waiters set up the best table near the water in anticipation of their noon entrance. Bunny Fay was wearing her beige linen by Oleg Cassini, and Lucretia Greer was wearing one of her summer classics by Mainbocher. They both kissed each other on their cheeks before settling down in their front row seats overlooking the harbor.

"Letty, you look absolutely divine today. I just love that color on you," Bunny began.

"Oh, thanks, and where did you get that scrumptious purse?"

"In Europe. A little shop on the Via Veneto in Rome. You like it?"

"Yes, it is so unique. It goes perfectly with your beige outfit. Cassini, right?"

"Good for you. Most of the women I know wouldn't know a Cassini from a Jacques Pennee," said Mrs. Fay using the insider's joke of calling the J.C. Penney's in Petoskey by a French name.

"How about a little knock?" asked Letty.

"Sure. Why not? Let's live it up. I'll have a Bloody Mary."

When the waiter came, Mrs. Greer ordered a very dry Martini for herself and a Bloody Mary for Mrs. Fay, her guest that day.

"What do you think about the new dues for the swimming pool?" asked Bunny. "George is livid."

"Well, I don't know. It might keep the riffraff out."

"What do you mean?" commented Bunny.

"That's how the riffraff got in." She was referring to MacCloud.

"Hum-m. You have a point there," said Letty Greer taking a long sip of her martini.

They both paused and looked over the lunch crowd. Nothing unusual, just the adult regulars with a few teenagers lounging around after the morning tennis lessons. The only new item was that Roger MacCauley was having lunch with Gina King.

"I see that 'Roger the Lodger' moved on," laughed Bunny.

"Must have been booted when Ambrose came back," Letty chuckled. Roger MacCauley was the perennial houseguest and moved from Harbor Point to Weque to Northport Point to Easthampton to Newport to Boca Raton to Palm Beach like a migrating bird. Many younger children called him "Uncle Roger."

"Letty, George and I are planning a little cruise on the 'Folly' next week. We thought we would go up to the 'Snows.' We would love to have you and Henry and Woody come along," asked Bunny.

"That sounds marvelous. You can count on Woody and I. Henry is a little harder to track down these days."

Bunny nodded and thought why did Letty have to marry that little hanger-on, Henry Greer. At least

he knows that everyone at the Point loathes him and
spends most of his time out in Wyoming at their
hunting lodge. He was such a neuter, but what could
you expect with Letty?

"Marvelous," said Bunny. "I'll tell George to notify
the captain and crew. Have you ever been to the
Cheneux Islands?"

"No, but I hear they are deserted and wonderful."

"Yes, you can skinny dip right off the boat. I don't,
but the girls do."

Letty was thinking that must delight the crew.

"So what are we having today?" asked Letty when
the waiter approached them. "I think I'll have the
tuna salad and another martini."

"Make mine the BLT, and I'll switch to iced tea."

They both relaxed in the warm sunlight and felt
that they had moved towards their mutual goal over
lunch. A late autumn wedding they both thought;
they did not feel they could risk waiting until
Christmas.

* * *

After the NM and Marlin races the crews would
head for the Little Harbor Club bar. During the
cocktail hour the younger group dominated while
the adults moved to the sidelines. Woody was holding
court at a table with a group of Derek's friends.

"And then after the final mission we would head
to Bangkok for R&R," he said.

"Bangkok? Bang cock?" laughed Jeff Haswell.

"That's what a friend of mine, George used to
say. He thought it was funny, too."

"It is funny. Banging your cock."

"Did I show you the photo of my girl who lived

there?"

"No," they clustered closer.

Woody opened up his wallet and spread all the contents on the table. Foreign driver's and pilot's licenses, military I.D.'s, a few photos, and a condom package lay on the table. He picked up the condom and stuffed it back in his wallet, before he picked out one photo from the rest. As he passed around the photo of May Ling in a suggestive pose, he received a nod of approval from the other young men.

Derek thought that the photo looked like the girl he saw Woody with on the Fourth of July in his speedboat. "She sure doesn't look like Bitsy," he said.

"No," Woody was surprised. "Why would she?"

"I dunno. Just that you're gonna marry Bitsy and everything."

"What? Have I ever told you that? Where did you get that crazy idea?"

"Everyone's talking about it."

"Who? Who is everyone?" They had never seen Woody so mad.

"All the grown-ups. The parents. Even your mother told my mother a couple of days ago."

"God damn it. It's not true. In fact I have someone else."

"Who?" They moved closer.

"None of your business," Woody stood up and walked to the bar.

Cliff was drying glasses and looking out the French doors at the calm harbor when Woody approached with a scowl on his face.

"Cliff, have you heard anything about my marrying Bitsy Fay?"

"Well, a few times."

"God damn gossips. Why don't they stick to their

own business?"

"Well, you must admit you have cut a high profile this summer."

"High profile? What do you mean?"

"Not only doing what you've been doing with Bitsy in the afternoons along with Evert and her sister . . ."

"How did you hear about that?"

Cliff just looked at the sun cast shadows on the large sand dunes at the end of Little Traverse Bay.

"Evert?"

Cliff nodded.

"Damn turkey. He doesn't know his head from his ass."

Cliff wiped another glass.

"Anyone else?"

"The other guys that Evert was bragging to."

"God. What a big mouth."

"That's not all."

"What do you mean? Not all."

"Some of the members of the board feel you are not a good influence on some of the young members. They are talking about reporting you to the Civil Air Patrol or someone for flying too low over the harbor."

"Damn old farts. Worse than the generals."

"Sorry, Woody."

"Not your fault, Cliff. You're just the messenger. Thanks for warning me," Woody stormed out of the bar.

He ran out, jumped in his speedboat, and roared across the placid evening harbor. Two board members, who were having cocktails on the terrace, looked at each other and nodded in agreement. Woody loosely moored the boat and running up the dock and stairs burst into the cottage.

His mother was sitting on the chintz sofa enjoying her solitary cocktail hour when he crashed through the doors.

"Woody? What the hell?" She sat upright shocked out of her reverie.

"Mother. What's all this about me and Bitsy Fay?"

"What do you mean?" Letty put on her most innocent face.

"About us getting married!"

"Well . . ."

"Well, what? I don't want to marry the girl. She turns me off."

"Well, that isn't what I heard," her eyes were narrowing.

"And what else have you heard?"

"That you weren't very discrete."

"What do you mean? Discrete."

"Well. They are just children. Minors."

"Bitsy is nineteen."

"But her sisters aren't. The younger one is just a child."

"But I didn't sleep with her sisters!"

"I know. But you did it right in front of them."

"How do you know that?"

"The little one told all of her friends at a slumber party."

"Oh, my god," he held his head.

"So you better marry Bitsy."

"I don't see the logic."

"Before she's pregnant."

"She's not going to be pregnant."

"Why not?"

"Mother, I'm not dumb."

"Oh. I see. You used protection?"

"Yes."

"Well, that's a relief."

"Mother, stop this marriage stuff. I have no intention of marrying Bitsy Fay. Never loved her, never will."

"Well, love isn't the most important . . ."

"Stop, Mother." He held up his hand. "It isn't going to happen."

"Oh, Woody, don't get so upset. And the Fays asked us on this marvelous cruise next week."

"Count me out."

"But I so looked . . ."

"You can go, but forget me."

"Are you sure?"

"Yes, I'm positive. It's a friend of mine's birthday, and I want to celebrate it."

"Anyone I know?"

"No. Not yet." He wheeled around and shot up the stairs to change.

Chapter G

Background Material
From the *History of the Ottawa and Chippewa Indians of Michigan*, pp. 90-96.

The south side of the straits, which now constitutes Emmet, Cheboygan, and Charlevoix counties, our tradition says, was exceedingly thickly populated by another race of Indians, whom the Ottawas called Mush-co-desh, which means, "the Prairie tribe." They were so called on account of being great cultivators of the soil, and making the woodland into prairie as they abandoned their old worn out gardens, which formed grassy plains. It is related, this tribe was quite peaceable, and were never known to go on a warpath. The Ottawas of Manitoulin had joined bands with them as their confederates. They called each other "brothers." But on one of the western war trips of the great Saw-ge-maw, who existed about the time America was first discovered by white men, he met with great disaster, as many of his warriors were killed; so on returning homeward with his remaining survivors, they crossed Little Traverse Bay in a canoe and approached the shores of Arbor Croche at the place now called Seven Mile Point, where there was a large village of Mush-co-desh. Saw-ge-maw said to his few warriors, "Let us take our sad news to our relations the Mush-co-desh." So as they approached the shore they began to make an unearthly wailing noise, according to the custom of the Ottawas, which was called the death song of the warriors. When the Mush-co-desh heard them they said to one another, "Hark, the Ottawas are crying. They have been marauding among some tribes in the west; but this time they have been worsted—good enough for them. See, they are coming ashore. Let us not permit them to land." So instead of preparing to join in their mourning, as would have been proper, they rashly determined to express their disapproval of the marauding expeditions and their contempt for those who engaged in them. Before Saw-ge-maw had fairly touched the beach, parties of Mush-co-desh ran down to the shore with balls of ashes wrapped up in forest leaves and with these they pelted Saw-ge-maw and his party as they came ashore. This treatment dreadfully provoked Saw-ge-maw, and the insult was

such as could only be wiped out with blood.
He told his warriors to pull homeward as
quickly as possible. "We will come back here
in a few days; we will not have to go so far
again to look for our enemies." Arriving at
Manitoulin Island, he immediately
prepared for a great war. After they were
completely equipped, they came back to the
southern peninsula of Michigan, stealthily
and carefully landing at the most
uninhabited part of the shore. They then
marched to one of the largest villages of
Mush-co-desh, which was situated between
Cross Village and Little Traverse, in a
beautiful valley in the northern part of the
township now called Friendship. Arriving
late in the afternoon within view of the
village, the Ottawas hid in ambush. One of
the old women of the Mush-co-desh was
going through the bushes looking for young
basswood bark from which to manufacture
twine or cord. She came right where the
Ottawas were lying in ambush. She was
terribly surprised, but the Ottawas
persuaded her not to reveal their presence
by telling her they would give her a young
man as her husband, pointing to one of the
best looking young warriors there. They told
her, early in the morning they were going
to fall upon the village and kill every one of
the Mush-co-desh, but when she heard the
war whoop she must run to them and she
should not be killed but be protected. The
foolish woman believed and kept the secret.
Early in the morning the war cry was heard,

and she ran to the Ottawas to be protected, but she was the first one to be slain. It was indeed a terrible calamity for the Mush-co-desh. At the beginning of the noise of massacre, the chief of the Mush-co-desh ran forward and screamed loud as he could, saying, "O! My father, Saw-ge-maw, what is the cause of your coming upon us so suddenly with death, as we have never wronged your race?" "Have you already forgotten" said Saw-ge-maw triumphantly, "that you have greatly insulted me on your borders? You have pelted me with ashes when I was lamenting over the loss of my braves." When the Mush-co-desh saw they could not prevail on Saw-ge-maw, nor could withstand an adversary so formidable and such well prepared warriors, they endeavored to flee, but they were overtaken and slaughtered. Only the swift-footed young men escaped, taking the sad message to other villages of Mush-co-desh, and as fast as the news reached them they fled with their women and children toward the south along the shore of Lake Michigan, and continued to fly, although they were not pursued by the Ottawas, till they reached the St. Joseph River, and there they stopped, and formed a union village, and began to cultivate the soil again.

The tradition says this was the greatest slaughter or massacre the Ottawas ever committed. The inhabitants of this village were probably from forty to fifty thousand. There were many other villages of Mush-co-

desh of minor importance everywhere
scattered through the northern part of the
southern peninsula of Michigan. Where
this doomed village was situated is yet to
this day distinctly visible, as there are some
little openings and trails not overgrown by
the forest.

Soon after this the Ottawas abandoned
their island and came over and took
possession of the country of the Mush-co-
desh. Most of them settled at the place now
called Magulpin's Point, where the present
lighthouse is situated, near old Mackinac.
At the time the French settled in Montreal,
Au-tche-a, one of the Ottawa prophets, told
his people there were some strange persons
living in this continent, who were far
superior to say other inhabitants upon the
earth. So Au-tche-a determined to search
for these wonderful people and he
persuaded five of his neighbors to
accompany him in his undertaking. They
started out, but they went a very roundabout
way, and it was a long time before they came
to the Ottawa River; then floating down they
came out on the St. Lawrence. They were
gone for more than a year. When they came
where the white men were, they first saw a
vessel or ship anchored in the middle of
the St. Lawrence, which they thought was a
monster waiting to devour them as they
came along. But as they neared it they saw
some people on the back of the monster. So
Au-tche-a and his party were taken on board,
and his little frail canoe was hoisted into

the ship. They found some Stockbridge Indians there also, who spoke a dialect of their language. After exchanging all they had, and learning how to handle firearms, they started back again to the straits of Mackinac. The tradition says, they arrived at their village on an exceedingly calm day, and the water was in perfect stillness in the straits. The Indians saw the canoe coming towards the shore of the village, when suddenly a puff of smoke was seen and a terrific clash of sound followed immediately. All the inhabitants were panic stricken, and thought it was something supernatural approaching the shore. But again and again they witnessed the same thing, as it came nearer and nearer. At last they recognized the great prophet Au-tche-a and his party coming back from his long trip, having found his "Manitou" that he was looking after. The reader may imagine how it was, when Au-tche-a landed and exhibited his strange articles—his gun with its belongings, his axes, his knives, his new mode of making fire, his cooking utensils, his clothing and his blankets. It was no small curiosity to the aborigines.

The Ottawas gradually extended their settlements towards the south, along the shore of Lake Michigan. The word Michigan is an Indian name, which we pronounce Mi-chi-gun, and simply means "monstrous lake." My own ancestors, the Undergrounds, settled at Detroit, and they considered this was the extent of their

possessions. But the greatest part of the
Ottawas settled at Arbor Croche, which I
have already related as being a continuous
village some fifteen miles long. But in the
forest of this country were not many deer,
and consequently when the winter
approached most of the Indians went south
to hunt, returning again in the spring
loaded with dry meat.

The Mush-co-desh were not long in
safety in the southern part of the state.
Intercourse had been opened between the
French and the Ottawas and Chippewas on
the straits of Mackinac and being supplied
with firearms and axes by the French
people, it occurred to the Ottawas that these
implements would be effective in battle.
Anxious to put them to the test, they
resolved to try them on their old enemies,
the Mush-co-desh, who had not yet seen the
white man and were unacquainted with
firearms. Accordingly an expedition was
fitted out. As the Ottawas approached the
village of their enemies, each carrying a gun,
the Mush-co-desh thought they were
nothing but clubs, so came out with their
bows and arrows, anticipating an easy victory.
But they soon found out that they were
mistaken. As the Ottawas came up they
suddenly halted, not near enough to be
reached by any arrows of Mush-co-desh, but
the Ottawas began to fire away with their
guns, poor Mush-co-desh; they suffered
more than ever in this second crushing
defeat. The Ottawas left only one family of

Mush-co-desh at this time and these went west somewhere to find a new home. My father and my uncles in their younger days while they were making a tour out west, happened to come across the descendants of this nearly annihilated tribe of Indians. They had grown to nine lodges only at that time, and they visited them in a friendly manner. The old warriors wept as they were conversing with them on their terrible calamities and misfortunes and their being once powerful allies and closely related; for these few still remembered the past, and what had become of their ancestors.

After the Ottawas took complete possession of the southern peninsula of Michigan, they fought some more tribes of Indians, subdued them, and compelled them to form confederation with them as their allies. Such as Po-to-wa-to-mies, Mano-me-mis, O-daw-gaw-mies, Urons and Assawgies, who formerly occupied Saw-ge-naw-bay. Therefore the word Saginaw is derived from the name Os-saw-gees, who formerly lived there. They have been always closely united with the Chippewas and very often they went together on the warpath, except at one time they nearly fought on account of a murder, as has been herein related. Also the Shaw-wa-nee tribe of Indians were always closely related to them.

But the Ottawa nation of Indians are always considered as the oldest and most expert on the warpath and wise councilors; and consequently every tribe of Indians far

and near, even as far as the Manitoba country,
out north, deposited their pipe of peace
with the head chief of the Ottawa nation as
a pledge of continual peace and friendship.
Every pipe of peace contained a short
friendly address which must be committed
to memory by every speaker in the council
of the Ottawas. If there was ever any outbreak
among these tribes who deposited their
pipe of peace with the head chief of the
Ottawa nation, a general council would be
called by the chiefs of the Ottawas, and the
pipe of peace belonging to the tribe who
caused the trouble would be lighted up,
and the short address contained in the pipe
would be repeated in the council by one of
the speakers. When the cause of the
outbreak or trouble was ascertained, then
reconciliation must be had, and friendly
relation must be restored, in which case
they almost invariably succeeded in making
some kind of reasonable settlement. This
was the custom of all these people; and this
is what formerly constituted the great
Algonquin family of Indians.

There are many theories as to the
origin of the Indian race in America, but
nothing but speculation can be given on
this subject. But we believe there must have
been people living in this country before
those tribes who were driven out by the
Ottawas and Chippewas, who were much
more advanced in art and in civilization, for
many evidences of their work have been
discovered. About two hundred and fifty

years ago, We-me-gen-de-bay, one of our
noted chiefs, discovered while hunting in
the wilderness a great copper kettle, which
was partly in the ground. The roots of trees
had grown around it and over it, and when
it was taken up it appeared as if it had never
been used, but seemed to be just as it came
from the maker, as there was yet a round
bright spot in the center of the bottom of it.
This kettle was large enough to cook a whole
deer or bear in it. For a long time the Indians
kept it as a sacred relic. They did not keep
it near their premises, but securely hidden
in a place most unfrequented by any human
being. They did not use it for anything
except for great feast. Their idea with
regard to this kettle was that it was made by
some deity who presided over the country
where it was found, and that the copper
mine must be very close by where the kettle
was discovered. One peculiarity of its
manufacture was that it had no iron rim
around it, nor ball for hanging while in use,
as kettles are usually made, but the edge of
the upper part was much thicker than the
rest and was turned out square about three-
fourths of an inch, as if made to rest on some
support while is use. When the Indians
came to be civilized in Grand Traverse
country, they began to use this "Mani-tou-
au-kick," as they called it, in common to boil
the sugar sap in it, instead of cooking bear
for the feast. And while I was yet at the
government blacksmith shop at the Old
Mission in Grand Traverse, they brought this

magical kettle to our shop with an order to
put an iron rim and ball on it so that it could
be hanged in boiling sugar, and I did the
work of fixing the kettle according to the
order.

From this evidence of working in metals
and from the many other relics of former
occupants, it is evident that this country has
been inhabited for many ages, but whether
by descendants of the Jews or of other
Eastern races there is no way for us to
determine.

Chapter VIII

WHITE CORVETTE

Woody was true to his word and picked up Trudy at the Indian Gift Shop after work on her birthday. She was glad to see him, because her parents had forgotten that it was her important eighteenth birthday. At least it was better than her sixteenth when she had been fishing with her father and his friends. She told them that she had always wanted to live on a deserted island like Robinson Crusoe. Her father dared her to get off on one of the deserted islands off of Waugoshaunce Point, and she did. The men got drunk, almost forgot her, and came back at dusk to pick her up. Almost anything would seem better than that birthday experience.

Don gave her a bonus, and Aunt Alice dropped by with a freshly baked chocolate cake, which Trudy shared with all of the customers who came in the store.

But Woody's face smiling and excited was her best present. He helped her into his red convertible and admired the green and white cotton dress she wore.

"Your eighteenth is important," Woody said.

"Uh-huh," Trudy watched the little town slip away, as they ascended the hill at the end of Main Street. She looked back over the deer park, over Wequetonsing, to the clear blue of the harbor with the slanted sunlight catching the water. Sailboats were going out for an evening race while a few yachts motored beyond the Point for a cocktail hour cruise.

Woody drove to Alanson where he turned off the main road to a gravel road. After about a mile and a half he came to a large, year-around house overlooking Crooked Lake. He pulled into the semi-circled driveway and honked. A middle-aged man appeared, motioned for Woody to follow behind him in the convertible, and walked down a wooded lane. Trudy wondered what was going on. They parked and got out of the car.

"Here we are," Woody said excitedly. "Trudy, this is Bob Glass, he is the owner of Glass Motors in Petoskey, the best Chevy-Olds dealership in northern Michigan."

Trudy smiled at him, as he opened the door to the wooden garage.

"Here it is!" Woody ran in.

The gloom of the garage hid the outlines of the tarpaulined shape in front of them. Bob and Woody unfastened some bindings and ropes to pull the tarp off a little white corvette.

"There she is," Woody said and gave Trudy a set of keys.

She looked at him questioningly.

"It's yours. It's your eighteenth birthday present. It's a 1953 original Corvette, number three off the line. Bob said I was the only man he'd sell it to."

Trudy looked at the car.

"Well, what do you say?"

Trudy gave him back the keys and walked back to the convertible.

"Trudy, what's the matter? Why are you crying?"

Trudy climbed into the convertible and turned away from him.

"Bob, I'll lock up here. Sorry to bother you. I'll have to spend a little time alone with her."

Bob walked back to his house letting the two lovers straighten out their tiff. He'd never seen a woman cry at a gift of a car before. Maybe they were just tears of joy.

"What's wrong, Trudy?" Woody put his arm around her.

"I don't need a car."

"Yes, you do."

"No. I walk to work."

"But wouldn't it be fun to just drive it."

"I don't know how."

"Oh, that's the problem. I'll teach you."

"No. Not the problem."

"What's the problem then?"

"I'm embarrassed." She began sobbing.

"Embarrassed?"

"Not your mistress," she choked it out.

"What?"

"Not a mistress."

"What do you mean, 'mistress'?"

"Mistress, mistress," she yelled.

"Beat's me. I thought you'd be happy. Any other

girl would be happy, if I gave them such a nice little corvette."

"I'm not any other girl."

"No, you're not. You're special and that's why I thought I'd make this a special birthday for you." He held her to him while she heaved in deep sobs. He could not figure her out. "But I thought you'd be happy."

"You don't respect me."

"I respect you."

"You just want to sleep with me."

"What?"

"Make me your mistress."

"What? Where did you get that idea?"

"Books."

"Books?"

"Movies."

"Movies? No, Trudy, I don't want to make you my mistress. I want to make you my wife."

Trudy stopped crying.

Woody realized what he had said.

Trudy looked away.

"Well," he said.

"No. No good."

"No good?" He was shocked now.

"No. I'm no good."

"No, Trudy, you're too good for me."

"Take me home."

"Trudy, I'm not taking you home. Not yet anyway."

That night Woody put over a hundred miles on his car. They drove to Charlevoix, then to Boyne City, to Horton Bay, then on back roads. They came to an agreement. He would register the Corvette in Trudy's name, but he would garage and drive it. He would teach her how to drive it. They would not talk about marriage.

*   *   *

"Trudy, you look sick," Don said when she went to work the next morning.

"I feel sick."

"Want to go home?"

"No, just tired."

Don let Trudy alone. He knew that she would talk when she was ready. In the late afternoon when no customers came in, and the flies buzzed in the dead hot air, she was ready to talk.

"Don, do you think I'm smart?"

"Of course, Trudy. I've always thought you were smart."

"Why can't I go to the University of Michigan?"

"I dunno. You tell me."

"They won't let me apply."

"Who?"

"The guidance counselor."

"Sounds strange to me."

"How come they let you apply? You're an Indian, too."

"Yes, but Trudy, I went on a football scholarship. They recruited me."

"Recruited you?"

"Yes," Don was embarrassed.

"Oh," Trudy was silent.

"Have your dress ready?" Don changed the subject.

"Sure."

"Bob Glass called today, and he wants Woody Woodward to drive the Indian Princess in the parade in his new white Corvette."

Trudy looked at him like a trapped animal.

"Probably be you."

She looked away.

"Why are Indians no good?" She asked.

"Trudy, how can you say such a thing."?

"Everyone says so."

"Who says so?"

"White folks. Aunt Alice's friends."

"They are just jealous. And guilty, too. We were here before them. We know things they will never know."

"I'm no good."

"Trudy, that's wrong. Dead wrong. You're the descendant of Chief Blackbird. You're the Indian royalty. You are noble and strong and smart. Don't you ever forget it."

Trudy smiled a shy smile for the first time all day.

"Remember Chief Blackbird was the postmaster here and wrote an Odawa/English/French dictionary for our people. He was wise and strong and never drank, like you. You look like him. Straight and strong."

"Really?"

"Yes, really. Now you leave early and get some sleep."

"Okay. Thanks, Don."

"Remember your bloodline."

"Okay."

*   *   *

The Pow-wow was the idea of some white promoters who saw a good business opportunity. They had organized and held the first annual Pow-Wow in Harbor Springs last summer, and it had been a big success. The promoters, the businesses in town, and the Chamber of Commerce all made a bundle. The Native Americans received little profit, yet they danced their native dances, sold handicrafts for a song, and were used as the marketing gimmick.

The Boosters were so happy that they built a large outdoor stadium, which was also used for football and baseball games by the high school. The program for this year featured the crowning of the Indian princess, the honorary naming of some prominent businessmen with their symbolic Indian names like "Great Eagle," in the Odawa language, and many native dances done by a band of professional Cherokees brought in by the organizers. Billy Tabeshaw and a group of Cross Village Odawas refused to perform and were planning their own pow-wow in Cross Village at the grounds of the Catholic Church.

Don was the lightening rod of all of this activity. He kept the different Native American groups from turning on each other, and he was diplomatic with the white businessmen and the outside promoters. But he was sad and discouraged the way his idea for tribal harmony and a method to raise money for the poorest members of his tribe had turned out. It was like a modern replay of his people's dealing with the white men. He did not think that he could ethically support it for a third year and would probably join Billy Tabeshaw and his group on their less ambitious project. He thought that at least the "Ottawa Indian Stadium" had come out of it, which was something for the whole town.

On the night of the Pow-Wow Trudy wore the white skinned fringed dress with leggings and moccasins, whose embroidery was repaired by her

mother and was fitted by her Aunt Alice. Don, as the
Chief, was able to arrange the gift of the dress as a
private donation to Trudy. Later at the stadium, Don
was right and crowned Trudy with a beautiful
headband and feather as the "Ottawa Indian
Princess." E.J. MacCloud, George Fay, and Ambrose
Pierce were all awarded honorary Odawa names of
strength and power.

After the ceremonies Woody waited for Trudy at
the top of the bluff overlooking the lighted stadium.

"God, you were beautiful down there," he said
helping her into her Corvette.

"Thanks," she was shining. "Where are we going?"

"I thought I'd take you out to the Point. A few
friends of mine are having a little party."

"On the Point?" Trudy was pleased, since this the
first time that Woody had taken her to Harbor Point.
And it was the first time he had introduced her to
any of his resort friends. She felt proud and happy.
"But I have to change clothes."

"Of course," he burnt rubber on the gravel
leading out to the paved road and fishtailed as he slid
on to the main street. Trudy thought that he would
ruin her car before she ever learned to drive it.

They went across the black harbor to the Point
in his speedboat, so that the guards at the gate never
knew that an Indian girl was on the Point in season
as a guest of an owner, or son of an owner. Woody
moored the boat at his family dock, and they walked
next door to the Haswell cottage. The senior Haswells
had to unexpectedly fly back to New York for the
funeral of a wealthy maiden aunt and more
important the reading of her will. Derek and Jeff
took advantage of their absence and invited their
friends over.

When Woody and Trudy arrived at midnight, a small group remained. The party had started at four in the afternoon and most had either passed out or gone to other parties. Woody opened the big-screened door and pulled Trudy into the wallpapered living room with Oriental rugs and original Impressionist paintings on the walls. The sound of rock and roll was coming from the dimly lighted den at the opposite side of the house.

When Woody and Trudy entered the den, several couples were making out on the couches, and others were slow dancing. Derek saw them enter and disengaged himself from one of the Smith twins.

"Woody," he staggered across the room where his friend, Woody, was standing with the girl he was with on the Fourth. "Welcome. Grab yourself a drink."

"Derek, I'd like you to meet Trudy. Trudy Mitchell. Derek Haswell."

The Smith twins propped themselves on their elbows and stared at Trudy. Then they looked at each other and left the room together laughing.

Trudy and Woody stood at the bar for awhile before they found an inconspicuous niche on the floor at the end of the couch where Debby Smith returned to the arms of Derek. Her twin sister, Bobby, was on the adjoining couch with another boy, and the two girls were talking to each other between bouts of kissing. Trudy became invisible. Woody held her hand and drank his drink. He was willing to lie low and see which direction the party took.

"Debby, you tell Derek the good news?" Said Bobby.

"No. Not yet."

"Want me to tell him?"

"Why not?"

"The rabbit is dead."

Derek sat up and looked at Debby. "You never told me."

"Guess not."

"My god. When did you. . . ?"

"We were over at the hospital this afternoon."

"But I never knew . . . I never knew that there was a possibility."

"Remember that time in the Marlin?"

"Oh, yeah."

"Well . . ."

"Debby, what would have happened?" Derek was whispering.

"Probably my mother would have called your mother, and they would have worked something out."

"Like what?"

"Eloping. Or my going to Europe to study for nine months and putting the baby up for adoption. Whatever."

"But I'm only seventeen," Derek was sitting up now.

"Big deal. I'm fifteen," she said.

Derek jumped to his feet and moved into the brightly lighted living room. Woody followed him. Trudy pushed further into her dark corner.

After awhile, Trudy could hear laughter and excited talk from the other room. Slowly all of the males went to see what was going on. Trudy was invisible. The Smith twins joined each other on one couch and whispered and laughed between themselves. They forgot Trudy. Everyone forgot Trudy. She curled into a ball and fell asleep.

A few hours later Woody woke her up, excited and full of energy.

"Come see what we have done." He pulled her to her feet and dragged her into the bright lights of the living room. On the floor between the different couples were cut-up sheets with ropes attached to them. Trudy surveyed the floor, the people, and then looked questioningly at Woody.

"Don't you see? They're parachutes."

The Haswell twins had taken their mother's best linen percale sheets and made parachutes of them with their friends.

"Oh," Trudy said. "What for?"

"To drop things from my plane tomorrow. I'll fly by the Little Harbor Club, and Derek will throw out the parachutes one by one."

"Oh," Trudy said.

"We can try to get some on the lawn. Maybe one in the pool. See, if they float." Woody was excited. Derek had forgotten Debby in his new project with Woody.

Woody, who had flown missions of mercy to Berlin and Dien Bien Phu, now almost saw these percale parachutes as bombs on his enemies, the old white men at the Little Harbor Club.

"I'm on a roll. Derek, mind if I used your phone?" Woody asked.

"No, why not? But who are you going to call at three a.m.?"

"The White House."

"The White House?"

"Yeah. Listen." Woody strode to the phone while Derek turned the music off. Everyone became quiet and moved towards the phone. Woody reached in his pocket, took out his wallet, and removed a card from it.

Woody dialed. Everyone held their breath.

"Hello, operator. This is an emergency call. This is Major Ernest Woodward, a Canadian R.A.F number 470986241. I need to talk to the White House."

He was standing, and everyone else was sitting. Trudy moved towards the door, ready to run.

"Yes, operator. I will wait."

Everyone took a sip of their drinks and relaxed a little.

"Woody, are you holding the button down?" Debby asked.

"No, come and see."

She looked and nodded to the group that he was not holding his thumb on the button.

"Yes, operator. Yes, this is Major Woodward. Hello, sir. Is this the war room? Could you identify yourself. Yes." He wrote something down. "Yes. Dovetail. Alpha. Yes, sir."

Woody put his hand over the receiver. "They are calling a general."

Trudy was frightened and signaled to him to hang up. The rest of the group was fascinated, even if drunk, like Woody.

"Yes, sir. Yes, sir. On a civilian mission at 1400 hours today, I sighted a suspicious plane near Sault Saint Marie. Looked like a glider, sir, but it had a motor. No, sir. No, sir. Never. No markings. Probably surveillance. Strange design. You're welcome. Anytime. Yes, sir. Will do."

Woody looked at the group and hung up. "They are going to wake up the President."

"Sure, Woody," one of the more drunken teenagers said.

"No, true. Or least what the General said."

"Did you see a suspicious plane today?" Debby asked.

"Maybe I did, and maybe I didn't. That will show the generals! Hey, turn on the music. I need another drink."

Woody became the life of the party. Everyone was asking him questions. Trudy waited in the dining room while a drunken boy told her the story of his life. The boy never asked her name or asked her one question about herself. She just listened and nodded.

At dawn the party broke up. They all ran for their boats or jumped on bicycles to race each other to their cars. They were all going to a pancake house that opened at 6:00 a.m. in Petoskey.

"I want to go home," Trudy said.

"Why? Aren't you hungry? I'm starved."

"I'd rather go home," she mumbled.

"Okay. Okay. I'll drop you off, but I'm going on with the rest of the gang."

"Fine."

*   *   *

Four hours later Trudy was awakened by a pounding at the door. They never had a doorbell. She had fallen asleep in her clothes and pushed her hair back, as she looked out the window to see a police car and a sheriff's car. She hurried down the steps.

When she opened the door, both Sheriff Drysdale and Chief Wampole were standing with serious expressions on their faces. She thought of Woody's phone call the night before.

"Trudy, can we speak to your mother? You can wait right here."

Irene Tabeshaw pulled on a housecoat. Her grey braid fell down her back. She was frightened when she came to the door.

"I'm afraid I have some bad news for you," Chief Wampole looked at the two scared American Indian women with the August morning sun falling on their faces. "Dick Mitchell is missing. He was on Elmer Post's fishing boat, and they were on their way to Beaver Island last night."

Irene and Trudy stared at him.

"Dick went fore to secure a loose line, and . . ."

A small child appeared between the two women.

"Well, they looked for him for hours in the dark. The Coast Guard is out now."

Trudy and Irene nodded.

*   *   *

All day the news was on the radio and television. Neighbors brought cakes and pies by. Someone took the children, even the nursing baby who was teething.

In the late afternoon Ben and Alice Mitchell joined the group of people sitting in the kitchen drinking coffee. Ben asked Trudy to step outside with him. They sat on the back porch steps.

"Trudy, you know your dad and I weren't too close."

Trudy nodded.

"Well, you are going to have to become the head of the family. If it's true, that is. You're grown-up now."

Trudy nodded again.

"What I have to tell you isn't such good news either."

Trudy stared at him waiting.

"Dick went down to the bank and borrowed on this house."

"How could he? It's mother's house."

"Well, he did. Used it as collateral."

Trudy did not know what he meant, but she knew it was not good.

"The bank called me this morning and apprised me of the situation. If Dick's gone and can't pay back his loans, they will have to sell the house. He didn't carry life insurance."

"But they weren't married."

"Common law after seven years."

"You mean he could get loans on mother's house without her even knowing about it?"

"You know how business is done in small towns. Just a handshake," he said proudly.

"Where will we go?"

"I don't know. Maybe you could move in with us for a while and help Alice around the house. She can't do the heavy work any more, and you are strong."

"But mom and the kids?"

"Oh, her relatives will probably take them in."

Trudy stared at the row of poplars that stood out against the hot August sky. She felt her insides shake like the shiny poplar leaves.

* * *

The Coast Guard looked for Dick Mitchell's body for three days before calling off the search. Irene was in a state of shock and could not cope with the kids. Trudy thought about quitting her job, but it was the only part of the day she enjoyed.

Woody asked her to join him at the Little Harbor Club. E.J. MacCloud had invited him and his date for dinner there. E.J. said that he had something important to talk about with Woody.

The Fay table went silent when Woody entered
the upstairs French doors of the Little Harbor Club
with Trudy on his arm, and they were shocked when
he joined the MacCloud table facing theirs.

"A traitor to his class," whispered Jimmy Jones to
Bunny Fay. "Who's the girl?"

"An Indian trollop he's been with lately," she
replied watching in horror as Woody pulled the girl's
chair out for her. He had always been so abrupt and
rude with Bitsy, who watched Woody with glassy eyes.
She could feel a blush coming over her face. She
had never felt so publicly humiliated before,
especially in front of her family and friends.

As E.J. MacCloud settled his porcine weight
into the end chair, he motioned for Woody to sit
on one side and Trudy on the other. MacCloud
knew how to play this for all it was worth. He saw
that the adventurous playboy escort of Bitsy Fay at
the beginning of the summer was madly in love
with a local Indian girl at the peak of the summer
season. Nothing could have pleased him more. He
turned to Trudy, instead of Woody who was
waiting.

"Trudy Mitchell, you made a charming princess
the other night."

"Thank you, Mr. MacCloud."

"I was really sorry to hear about your father. Any
news?"

"No, the Coast Guard didn't find anything."

"What a shame. What a shame. That damn Post.
He takes that little fishing skiff out to Beaver Island
every weekend without running lights, and I heard
he didn't even have enough life vests. If only Dick
had a life vest on . . ."

Trudy was glad to talk to someone who was from

Petoskey and knew the same people she did. She relaxed.

"Woody, you know you're with royalty here. No one better to have in your bloodline, than Chief Blackbird."

Woody was surprised by the attention MacCloud was giving Trudy. He thought he had misjudged the man.

"Yup, Chief Blackbird was tops in my book. How's your mother holding up?"

"Not good." Trudy wanted to tell him about the bank, but she had not even told Woody.

"Let me know, if there's anything I can do to help. Okay, Trudy?"

She nodded.

E.J. MacCloud turned to Woody now and watched Bitsy Fay get up and leave the club with her mother. George Fay glared at him. MacCloud was happier then he had been all summer.

"Now, Woody, what are you planning to do this fall?"

"Haven't made up my mind yet." Woody felt as if he was losing his internal gyroscope and needed a focus, a mission, a project, self-discipline, even a job.

"Jack told me you might be open to joining our team. Jack's the best in the business."

"He's a fine pilot," Woody said.

"He's the best. Flew President Hoover."

"Sure," Woody thought that was a long time ago, and Jack was drinking too much tonight before flying the company plane to New York tomorrow. Woody did not drink in front of MacCloud.

MacCloud was thinking the same thing and that is why he wanted Woody as a back up. MacCloud had checked out Woody's flying history, but he was not current with Woody's excessive drinking that summer. MacCloud spent too much time in the air not to have the best that money could buy, and he felt that was Woody Woodward.

"Why don't you fly with us for awhile. You must be bored dropping parachutes on the club."

"Yeah," Woody was embarrassed of what boredom and anger had driven him to do. "I could use a mission. How would it work?"

"Two weeks on and two weeks off. I'll match what you made in Germany or Indochina. Okay?"

"Sounds good. When do I start?"

"Whenever you are ready. It's your call."

They all toasted to Woody's affiliation with the MacClouds. Mr. Fay rounded up the last of his guests and left, so that he did not have to watch the boars at MacCloud's table drink the good Mouton Rothschild like it was soda. He would never forgive Woody Woodward and how he had treated his daughter, and he never even knew they had slept together. Mrs. Fay had guessed and had recently taken Bitsy and Sudsy to the doctor for birth control. She did not want any mistakes in her family like what she expected to soon hear about the Indian girl with Woody now. George Fay vowed to himself to get the board to blackball Woody from the club and report his dangerous flying stunts.

Chapter H

From the *History of the Ottawa and Chippewa Indians of Michigan,* pp. 15-18.

Cases of Murders Among the Ottawas and Chippewas Exceedingly Scarce—Ceding the Grand Traverse Region to the Chippewas on Account of Murder—Immorality Among the Ottawas not Common—Marriage in Former Times.

The murders in cold blood among the Ottawas and Chippewa nations of Indians in their primitive state were exceedingly few, at least there was only one account in our old tradition where a murder had been committed, a young Ottawa having stabbed a young Chippewa while in dispute over their nets when they were fishing for herrings on the Straits of Mackinac. This nearly caused a terrible bloody war between the two powerful tribes of Indians (as they

225

were numerous then) so closely related. The tradition says they had council after council upon this subject, and many speeches were delivered on both sides. The Chippewas proposed war to settle the question of murder, while the Ottawas proposed compromise and restitution for the murder. Finally the Ottawas succeeded in settling the difficulty by ceding part of their country to the Chippewa nation, which is now known and distinguished as the Grand Traverse Region. A strip of land which I believe to have extended from a point near Sleeping Bear, down to the eastern shore of the Grand Traverse Bay, some thirty or forty miles wide, thence between two parallel lines running southeasterly until they strike the head waters of Muskegon River, which empties into Lake Michigan not very far below Grand Haven. They were also allowed access to all the rivers and streams in the Lower Peninsula of Michigan, to trap the beavers, minks, otters and muskrats. The Indians used their furs in former times for garments and blankets. This is the reason that to this day the Odjebwes (Chippewas) are found in that section of the country.

It may be said, this is not true; it is a mistake. We have known several cases of murders among the Ottawas and Chippewas. I admit it to be true, that there have been cases of murders among the Ottawas and Chippewas since the white people knew them. But these cases of murders occurred some time after they came in contact with the white races in their country; but I am speaking now of the primitive condition of Indians, particularly of the Ottawas and Chippewas, and I believe most of those cases of murders were brought on through the bad influence of white men, by introducing into the tribes this great destroyer of mankind, soul and body, intoxicating liquors! Yet, during sixty years of my existence among the Ottawas and Chippewas, I have never witnessed one case of murder of this kind, but I heard there were a few cases in other parts of the country, when in their fury from the influence of intoxicating liquors.

There was one case of sober murder happened about fifty years ago at Arbor Croche, where one young man disposed of his lover by killing, which no Indian ever knew the actual case of. He was arrested and committed to the Council and tried according to the Indian style; and after a long council, or trial, it was determined the murderer should be banished from the tribe. Therefore, he was banished. Also, about this time, one case of sober murder transpired among the Chippewas of Sault Ste. Marie, committed by one of the young Chippewas whose name was Wau-bau-ne-me-kee (White Thunder), who might have been released if he had been properly tried and impartial judgment exercised over the case, but we believe it was not. This Indian killed a white man, when he was perfectly

sober, by stabbing. He was arrested, of
course, and tried and sentenced to be hung
at the Island of Mackinac. I distinctly
remember the time. This poor Indian was
very happy when he was about to be hung
on the gallows. He told the people that he
was very happy to die, for he felt that he was
innocent. He did not deny killing the man,
but he thought he was justifiable in the sight
of the Great Spirit, as such wicked monsters
ought to be killed from off the earth; as this
whiter man came to the Indian's wigwam in
the dead of night, and dragged the mother
of his children from his very bosom for
licentious purpose. He remonstrated, but
his remonstrances were not heeded, as this
ruffian was encouraged by others who stood
around his wigwam, and ready to fall upon
this poor Indian and help their fellow
ruffian; and he therefore stabbed the
principal party, in defense of his beloved
wife, for which cause the white man died. If
an Indian should go to the white man's
house and commit that crime, he would be
killed; and what man is there who would say
that is too bad, this Indian to be killed in
that manner? But every man will say amen,
only he ought to have been tortured before
he was killed; and let the man who killed
this bad and wicked Indian be rewarded!
This is what would be the result if the Indian
would have done the same thing as this white
man did.

The Ottawas and Chippewas were quite
virtuous in their primitive state, as there

were no illegitimate children reported in our old traditions. But very lately this evil came to exist among the Ottawas—so lately that the second case among the Ottawas of Arbor Croche is yet living. And from that time this evil came to be quite frequent, for immorality has been introduced among these people by evil white persons who bring their vices into these tribes.

In the former times or before the Indians were christianized, when a young man came to be a fit age to get married, he did not trouble himself about what girl he should have for his wife; but the parents of the young man did this part of the business. When the parents thought best that their son should be separated from their family by marriage, it was their business to decide what woman their son should have as his wife; and after selecting some particular girl among their neighbors, they would make up quite a large package of presents and then go to the parents of the girl and demand the daughter for their son's wife, at the same time delivering the presents to the parents of the girl. If the old folks say yes, then they would fetch the girl right along to their son and tell him, We have brought this girl as your wife so long as you live; now take her, cherish her, and be kind to her so long as you live. The young man and girl did not dare to say aught against it, as it was the law and custom amongst their people, but all they had to do was to take each other as man and wife. This was all the rules and ceremony of getting married in former times among the Ottawas and Chippewas of Michigan; they must not marry their cousins or second cousins.

CHAPTER IX

SWEETGRASS AND SMOKE

The night that Woody and Trudy joined MacCloud at the Little Harbor Club was important for both of them. Trudy had ventured into the Little Harbor Club and was not turned into a pillar of salt, although she would never be accepted there as a pillar of society. Woody was delighted how MacCloud and his crew welcomed, even revered Trudy. When he accepted the offer by MacCloud, Woody had a hidden agenda. Trudy had said that it was crazy to talk about marriage when he did not have a job, not knowing that he could buy and sell most of the stores and companies in Harbor Springs. He also knew that she did not want the "togetherness" being promoted by the women's magazines of the day. If he were gone for two weeks and home two weeks, neither of them would feel constrained or bored.

Woody drove to a spot on the bluff and parked

the Corvette. The first cluster of lights in the darkness
was Harbor Springs, the second line of lights out on
the black water was Harbor Point, and the bank of
lights in the distance crowned by the radio towers
was Petoskey. Woody had his arm around Trudy on
the chilly night.

"So Sweetgrass, you knocked them dead
tonight."

"Uh-huh."

"MacCloud certainly liked you."

"He's okay."

"What about my new job?"

"Good."

"Want to change your mind?"

"About what?"

"About marrying me."

"Maybe." Trudy felt good about holding her own
at the Little Harbor Club and being respected about
being Chief Blackbird's descendant.

"Maybe? That's great news. For you that's almost
a 'yes'." He hugged her to him.

"But my dad . . ." Her face fell.

"I know. But what can we do? I've flown the area
every day and haven't seen a trace."

"When we know that he is gone, then we can get
married."

"We may never know. Lake Superior doesn't give
up bodies, you know?"

"This is Lake Michigan." She expected Dick
Mitchell to appear any night, drunk and having
played a trick on them. When he appeared, the bank
would let them keep the house, and everything
would be the way it always was. Then she would go to
the University of Michigan in person and try to get
in. Maybe Don would drive her down there. She

would leave her parents' house with her father home and go to college. She never told Woody of her plans.

But fate had different plans for Trudy, because one night on a dead calm night around sunset Derek Haswell and a group of other teenagers in his wooden boat on the way up the shore to a beach party at Five Mile Creek, saw a lump floating in the calm water. When they pulled their boat over to it, they realized that it was a dead body. It was lying face down in the water and when Derek turned it over with grappling hooks, he recognized Dick Mitchell from the Pier Bar. The body was white and bloated, and fish had eaten off an ear and his fingers.

The group of Derek's friends pulled and moved the body of Dick Mitchell into the dingy and slowly towed it back to the harbor. One of the speedboats in the Haswell flotilla hurried ahead to the Coast Guard office next to the city dock. By the time the Haswell boat with the dinghy in tow rounded the Point over a dozen boats had heard the news and were circling the speedboat. Derek brought his boat next to the city dock, and people brought the dinghy alongside the large dock with the grappling poles. When the motion of the large wooden boat stopped, and the dinghy was secured, the smell of the body reached the onlookers' nostrils. Two people ran to the opposite side of the dock and threw up into the water. Carp rose and had a feast.

*　　*　　*

The funeral was held at the family plot in the Harbor Springs cemetery, on the hill overlooking Little Traverse Bay. The day was windy and overcast with the heavy-bellied clouds which announced a coming Labor Day and autumn. Dick's drinking buddies and their families were all there, as well as the Tabeshaw's. Two well-dressed men from the bank were in attendance and afterwards approached Irene Tabeshaw to give her an envelope.

At that moment Trudy forgot any immediate plans for college and decided to marry Woody, who was standing next to her, as soon as she could.

Chapter I
From *Michigan Prehistory Mysteries,* p. 125.

One historical accounting states that Father Charlevoix wrote in a letter to the King of France, that war captives were often sacrificed upon this big boulder. On one specific occasion he described a 15 year old girl was offered up to appease the "manitou." The Indians tied the maiden to the stone, built and lit a huge fire all around the rock. Then as the flames climbed higher, the leader or chief fired an arrow into the girl's heart. Almost at once the warriors rushed forward and dipped their arrowheads in her blood to make themselves invincible!

*   *   *

From *Along With Youth*, p. 53.

At the end of the first week in May, a
wire arrived in Oak Park to notify Ernest
that he was to report to the headquarters of
the Red Cross in New York on May 13.
Clarence immediately wired Ernest at
Seney, Michigan. According to family legend, the Indian runner who worked for the
telegraph office took three days to locate
Ernest and his friends. However it was,
Ernest returned to Oak Park just in time to
pack his things. Up north he had learned
that Prudence Bolton, three months pregnant by a French-Canadian lumberjack, had
committed suicide. Both had taken strychnine, the Indians said, and their screams
had been heard for hours across Susan Lake.

*   *   *

From *Petoskey Evening News*, front page headline on February 15, 1918.

NORTHERN MICHIGAN BURIED UNDER HEAVY FALL OF SNOW

WORST STORM OF PRESENT WINTER
IN THIS REGION AND ROADS AND
RAILROADS ARE BLOCKED. TWELVE

INCHES OF THE BEAUTIFUL PILES IN
BIG DRIFTS BY FIERCE GALE.

PERE MARQUETTE TRAINS ARE
STALLED IN DRIFTS NEAR
CHARLEVOIX WHILE C.R. & I. TRAIN IS
DELAYED BY DERAILMENT AT
ALANSON. TELEGRAPH WIRES BRO-
KEN DOWN NEAR CLARION.

Railroad men say last night's
storm of snow and wind was the worst
of the winter so far as halting traffic is
concerned. The storm broke at it's
heaviest just after 5 o'clock and continued for several hours. The wet
snow, almost like rain, was driven before a fierce northeast wind and piled
in huge drifts everywhere. The north-
bound Pere Marquette passenger
train ran into one of these drifts near
Charlevoix and was buried there all
night and most of today. A relief train
from Traverse City was sent to pull
her out but this train also became
stalled in the drifts.

This forenoon a flanger being sent
south over the G.R.&I., struck a switch
point just north of the Alanson station
at 10 o'clock and left the rails. The
southbound passenger train was sent

back to Brutus to wait until the tracks were cleared and placed in repair. The snow plow, which was sent north over this road last night, did not get out ahead of the passenger train.

The Harbor Springs run was made with great difficulty. The train became stalled at the Petoskey station on her return trip and had to be dug out by the section crew.

Telegraph wires are reported in bad shape near Clarion and at points north of Petoskey.

Manager Williams of the telephone company reports the storm was the worst from Cadillac north along the G. R. & I. and from Ellsworth north along the Pere Marquette.

Rain and sleet is reported at points farther south but the snow evidently hit only the north half of the state.

*   *   *

From *Petoskey Evening News,* February 15, 1918, inside page.

CHARLEVOIX MAN AND WOMAN COMMIT SUICIDE THERE FRIDAY MORNING

Richard Castle of Charlevoix, and a young Indian girl with whom he had been living, committed suicide this morning at about 7 o'clock at the home of Castle's father at Charlevoix. They took strychnine. Castle was recently convicted of assault on one Joe Brock, with intent to commit robbery.

Castle had been under arrest since last August, when with Ruth Blaine, of Charlevoix. The Blaine girl was convicted last fall in circuit court and on December 16, last, committed suicide by hanging herself to the door of her cell in the Charlevoix county jail. Castle was out on bond awaiting sentence.

Chapter X

TWO DIFFERENT WORLDS

Trudy decided to consult her Aunt Alice about her wedding. Aunt Alice always knew what was right and what was wrong.

"Now, Trudy, are you sure you know what you are doing?"

"But Aunt Alice, I'm eighteen."

"But isn't this a bit sudden?" Alice wondered if Trudy was expecting after all.

"Not really. I've been waiting a lifetime."

"Not to get married. You said that you'd never get married."

"No, but to leave Harbor Springs. See the world. Live in a nice house."

"Mrs. Henshaw always says to 'marry the lifestyle, not the man.' Sounds like that's what you've chosen."

"No. But why did you want me to marry Johnnie Moore, but not Woody?"

"Johnnie offered security. You would know where you would be ten, twenty years ahead with him. You could count on him."

"That's what I hated about him. He was so dull. So secure. By 'security' you mean money, don't you?"

"Not necessarily," Alice was ruffled, because it was exactly what she and her women friends meant. They only approved of 'secure' marriages like their own where the women did not have to work, but stayed at home with the children. "And what about children. Have you thought about that?" She still thought that was the motivating factor.

"Yes. I've thought a lot about children. I would like to have Woody be the father of my children. I think he would dote on them like he does on me. But I want children when I'm ready, not forced on me, not accidents . . ." Her voice trailed off, as she thought about her brothers and sisters. She could feel cubs in a den with Woody. She could see the protective glint in his eyes.

"You know people say that Woody is crazy," said Aunt Alice.

"Crazy?" Trudy could not help but think of the Patsy Cline song.

"Yes. Wild. Crazy."

"How?"

"He was always such a quiet little boy, but when he came back this summer he has been acting crazy."

"How?"

"Flying that plane all over. He's a hazard. I heard he was flying it upside down past Forest Beach."

"Oh, is that all. Woody's a good pilot." She relaxed.

"Do you fly with him?"

"No."

"Why not?"

"I've been working." She lied, not about working, but about the fact that she turned down Woody's invitations to fly. Because she was not ready to die yet. She did not know whether drowning in the cold dark waters of Lake Michigan like her father, or crashing in a light plane with Woody would be worse.

"Then there's the other thing," Alice added.

"What other thing?"

"Maybe I shouldn't tell you," said Alice looking away from Trudy's trusting eyes. "Oh, never mind."

"No. What other thing?"

Alice pondered her options thinking that "Ignorance is bliss," but then again the girl is planning to marry him. So she blurted it out: "With the Fay girls."

"What do you mean?" Trudy knew that Woody was dating Bitsy Fay before her. She had even watched them together on the day she brought Mrs. Fay's dress to Harbor Point.

"All of them. Mrs. Henshaw told me. And the little one's so young. Just a child."

Already the story had changed from the first time Mrs. Henshaw heard it.

"What?" Trudy's pupils dilated.

"He had sex with all of them. 'Jail bait,' Mrs. Henshaw said, 'sick.'"

"No, I don't believe it," Trudy said.

"Believe what you want. You're the one has to live with him." Alice's chest puffed up like a white leghorn hen.

"No. It's not true," said Trudy, but she thought that even if it is true, it happened before I met him. Trudy had the deluded thought patterns of most women who think that a man miraculously changes the minute that they meet. Most women start the meter on their first meetings, and their ego makes them think that a man will change and lose all of his previous bad habits under their influence. But Trudy had decided to marry Woody for better, not worse, and richer, not poorer, until she did not need him anymore or one of them died. She had no intention of letting Alice's story turn her from the course she had set. Trudy also knew that as Woody's wife she would have a better chance of continuing her education, going to college. Maybe she would earn a B.A., maybe even a Ph.D.

"Woody's mother won't allow your wedding. I just know she won't." Alice added.

"But what about the wedding?" Trudy wanted to get her aunt back on track.

"Well," Alice came back to her positive self and was in her element. "We can make a nice organza white dress from some patterns in one of my books. You will be married in the Methodist Church, of course. Sarah Maynard can play the organ. Then afterwards we can have everyone up here for the reception. I can bake the bridal cake."

"Oh, Aunt Alice. I knew that I could count on you." Trudy leapt up and hugged her aunt.

"We must put an engagement photo in the paper. You can use your high school graduation picture. You know a woman only has her name in print twice: when she is married and when she dies."

"Oh, Aunt Alice, you contradicted yourself. What about the engagement picture or the birth of her children or if she wins the Nobel Prize?"

"Oh, Trudy, you are such a dreamer!" answered Alice.

The next week was a busy one. Since Trudy

insisted on working at the store despite all of the
wedding plans. She wanted to be married on Labor
Day weekend, but the church was already booked.

Woody did not want to tell his mother about his
plans, but decided to introduce Trudy to her. He
thought that Trudy would win her over.

"Mother, I'd like to have someone over to dinner
tomorrow night."

"Oh, good. Is it Bitsy? Have you made up?"

"No, it isn't."

"Oh, then is it that nice Derek Haswell? You have
been spending a lot of time with him lately."

"No, mother, it is a girl I've been seeing."

"Who?" She looked at him suspiciously. Woody
never had invited one girl by herself to dine with
them.

"Prudence Mitchell."

"Prudence Mitchell. Who is she?"

"She lives in Harbor Springs. Her father was the
one who drowned last week. Derek found the body."

"Oh, yes, I heard something about that. Fine, just
tell Clara." She relaxed. Woody was always feeling
sorry for people and helping them out. That must
be it.

Even as a little boy he bonded with the help, she
thought. He was always for the outsider, the
underdog. Maybe he feels a little that way himself,
she thought.

When Trudy arrived in the speedboat with Woody
for the dinner with his mother, she wore his favorite
green and white dress. She was feeling good until
she stepped on the dock and saw Woody's mother
on the front porch. She was one of the blonde older
women who were always so rude to her in the store.
She had dealt with her many times before. Trudy

wanted to turn and jump back in the Chris-Craft. Nothing was worth this, she thought.

Letty Greer gave the little Indian tramp her best fish eye look. She had called some of her friends to check the girl out and found that Woody had been having an affair with her for over a month or that is what her friends said. All those late nights, she thought. She had seen the little gold digger in town at the Indian store. She certainly did not look forward to this dinner. Woody was thinking with his dick not his head, she thought. Men are so stupid.

When they reached the top step, Woody tried to introduce Trudy to his mother, but Letty just turned away and went into the house. He noticed that her step was uneasy. She had been drinking.

They all sat down in the overstuffed living room, and Joseph came out to take their drink orders. Trudy asked for a Coke, and Woody decided he needed a double while his mother had another martini. Trudy sat upright, as Mrs. Greer critically looked at her white sandals and cotton dress which now seemed shabby to Trudy.

"Mother, Trudy works at the Indian Gift Shop," said Woody.

"Yes, I know," she said looking out the window and lighting a cigarette.

"She was valedictorian of her class."

"Where, might I ask?"

"Harbor Springs High."

"Oh. How interesting," she said flatly.

A boat horn sounded over the water. The church bells pealed at six p.m. The silence in the living room was made more obvious by the crashing of the waves on the Little Traverse Bay side of the house. Trudy crossed her legs and folded her arms.

"Woody, how about another drink?" His mother handed him her glass.

"Mother, you shouldn't."

"Don't tell me what to do, young man." She glared at him and her mouth set in a hard line. Her lipstick had run up the cracks lining her pinched mouth.

Woody sighed and fixed her another drink. His mother yawned in Trudy's face.

"Mother, I wanted you to meet Trudy, because we are going to get married."

"What!" She wheeled on him and then stared at Trudy's stomach.

"Yes, in a few weeks in the Methodist Church in town. I hope you will come."

"No. I won't come, because there will be *no* wedding. Woody, have you lost your senses?"

"I've never felt more sure of my senses in my whole life."

"Is she pregnant?" Mrs. Greer talked about Trudy, as if she were not there.

"No." Woody's face set. His teeth began to show, as his lips pulled back. He could feel the hair stand up on his arm.

"Well, that's good. Then why all of this silly talk of a wedding?"

Woody went and sat next to Trudy on the couch, as she remained frozen, trying to be invisible.

"Mother, this is the woman I love, and I'm going to marry her, whether you like it or not."

"Woody, I absolutely forbid this." Mrs. Greer stood and towered over them.

"Mother, don't do this." Woody jumped to his feet and faced off against her.

"I will. And you won't get a bloody cent! At least from me."

"Sorry, Mother, too late for that. The trust fund is locked up. Besides I have a job."

"A job? With who?"

"E.J. MacCloud. Flying the company plane."

"Oh, my god. You *have* lost your mind. Woody, what has come over you? Didn't I teach you anything?"

"Yes, you did, mother. All the wrong things. Trudy and I are leaving now. We're not staying for dinner." He pulled Trudy behind him and slammed out the door.

*　　*　　*

When Woody brought Trudy home that night, she invited him in to meet her mother for the first time. Irene Tabeshaw sat in the kitchen with Billy Tabeshaw. They were drinking iced tea. Billy was pleased to see them when they entered the room.

"Hi, Trudy. Hi, Woody," he said.

Irene was flustered meeting Woody who she had heard so much about.

"Mom, this is Woody. Hi, Billy." Trudy went to get two glasses and the pitcher of iced tea. They pulled two chairs up to the table.

"Nice to finally meet you, Mrs. Mitchell," said Woody.

Irene Tabeshaw looked thankful for the respectful address.

"Sorry to hear about your husband."

"Thanks."

"It just gets worse," Billy said.

"What do you mean?" asked Woody.

"Bank wants to take Irene's house away."

"How?"

"Dick had loans on it. Now they want money or sell the house."

"How much?" asked Woody.

"Seven thousand five hundred."

Trudy's eyes opened. She had not realized it was that much. Irene began crying again.

"I'll pay it," said Woody.

Irene and Billy looked at him in disbelief. Trudy smiled.

"Trudy and I are getting married. Just look at this as a little down payment on the bride," Woody said and thought that the amount was close to what he had paid for May Ling.

"You can't do this," said Irene who was proud. Trudy put her hand on her mother.

"We are family," said Woody. "That's what family is for."

Irene began sobbing again. Billy and Trudy held her as Woody left.

*   *   *

E.J. MacCloud invited the engaged couple over to his house. He had a surprise for them, and he loved surprises, especially when he was the giver, and people became indebted to him. This couple was a gift from heaven for his social aspirations.

Trudy and Woody drove to the house on Glenn Drive which was different than all the other houses and cottages in the area. On the horse and buggy tour of Harbor Point and the nearby area which carried tourists from the railway station throughout the town, the MacCloud house was described as "a California style beach house built from prefab materials where Clark Gable was once a house guest."

All of which was true. Clark Gable was picked up on the MacCloud plane in Ohio when he was visiting his relatives, and Gable and his relatives enjoyed a long weekend at the MacCloud place. MacCloud knew many movie stars in Palm Springs.

When Trudy and Woody walked into the rambling, one story beach house, they entered a Hollywood set. The decor was white with mirrors and views of the enveloping sand dunes and lake. You took your shoes off when you walked on the thick, pure white rugs. No one but MacCloud's Palm Springs decorator would have furnished a rustic beach house in northern Michigan this way, but again the house was featured in several glossy magazines to the delight of both the client and the decorator.

MacCloud, his unassuming, but pretty wife, Ella, and Jack were there to greet Trudy and Woody. Two Asians of undetermined origins were serving drinks and Beluga Caviar canapés. After they settled down, Woody talked to the servants in several languages and determined that they were Hong Kong Chinese. MacCloud was impressed.

"Nice day," said Jack.

"High cirrus. Not much wind," answered Woody.

Ella MacCloud moved to sit near Trudy. She liked the young girl and knew what a difficult situation she was in. She knew what it was like to be young and poor. She had married MacCloud for a mink coat and never expected him to come this far.

"Have you set a date?" Ella MacCloud asked.

"Well, we are trying, but the church isn't available," answered Trudy.

"When do you want to get married?" asked E.J.

"Labor Day weekend." Trudy squeezed Woody's hand.

"Soon," frowned MacCloud.

Trudy nodded.

"Well, we might be able to arrange that. What do you say, Ella?"

She nodded.

"Okay, you two. I have a proposition to put to you. Okay?"

They both nodded.

"We just bought a bigger plane, and I want to take it to Europe before the weather turns. I'll need Woody on duty for about a month. Trudy, I thought I'd take you along and call it your honeymoon. Okay?"

Trudy was delighted, and Woody was pleased by her excitement. He had not seen her so happy, since before Dick's death.

"That's not all," MacCloud said, feeling as if he were making Trudy "Queen for a Day," like the popular T.V show. "We will throw the wedding and reception at my Beach Club on Labor Day weekend. I'm having a wild boar flown in from California anyway, and Jose is going to do a luau for me. Might as well get a Justice of the Peace there and make it a wedding feast. Kill two birds with one stone."

Trudy's face darkened as she thought about her mother, all of the Tabeshaws, and Aunt Alice who would not fit in with MacCloud's racy crowd.

"Trudy," MacCloud continued. "I am just having it be a family barbecue for my family and relatives from Petoskey. I'm sure that they know most of your family."

Trudy gave him a thankful smile.

"Thank you. Thank you so much," she said.

Woody gave her a big hug.

*   *   *

On the day of the wedding, Trudy woke up in her bedroom and knew that she would never spend another night here. She looked around, as if she were seeing it for the first time or allowing herself to see it as it really was, not through the filter of her book filled mind. The yellow paint that she had put on herself two years ago was beginning to peel. The army cot with the squeaking springs and old mattress was painted a dark blue, and it, too, was peeling. The single bulb dangling from the center of the room with the shade she bought from the five and dime was swinging in the breeze that blew out the white organdy curtains she still liked. The college catalogs in the corner and the books all around gave the room the cluttered look of a teenager's room. She was grown-up now, about to be married. But, in reality, felt that she had never been a child. As the oldest by far in her family, she felt as if she were the co-parent with Irene while Dick was some kind of undisciplined teenager. She was glad to leave the house, but she would not let herself think about the "crazy" side of Woody.

Against the protests of Aunt Alice, who was disappointed that she was not orchestrating the wedding after all, Trudy had decided to be married in her Indian Princess garb, not the white girl's dream white wedding dress. She would never have felt comfortable in a frilly, ruffled Southern Belle wedding dress like the one that Aunt Alice had in mind. She would play the role of Indian Princess once more, only this time at her own wedding.

Trudy was also happy to be married outdoors and on the beach where she was at home. She had never told Alice, but she had always felt out of place as the only Indian at the Methodist Church. Now she would be under the wide sky, and a Justice of the Peace would just make it legal, not a production. No bridesmaids, no ushers, no father, Trudy was just going to step up next to Woody and become his wife, but she felt like a virgin sacrifice.

Woody hired two horse and buggies that usually took guests out to the Point and had them pick up the Tabeshaws in Indian town to go to the Beach Club. This was the first time that they rode in the buggies, behind the large horses stabled down the street where they lived. Usually only summer people rode in the carriages. The rest of Trudy's relatives walked or drove like Ben and Alice Mitchell.

MacCloud had bought the land at the end of Glenn Drive and had tried to start a Beach Club, but few people would join. The empty cabanas lined the water. The land was described in the popular 1910's best seller, *The Indian Drum*. The Indians all knew that it was located on sacred land and that anyone who built and lived on it was cursed. Trudy felt protected there, but white friends from high school felt that the area was spooky. One said that a white owl flew directly at him, in daylight, and he had to run. The owl followed him all the way back into town on the road through the swamp which lead into Indian town.

When Trudy arrived at the Beach Club in the horse and carriage with her mother and brothers and sisters, the boar was roasting in the pit in the sand. The flames were so high that they seared the lower branches of a red pine nearby. MacCloud's guests numbered around thirty with his Scottish relatives from Petoskey, Cliff and Joyce, Jack, and a few business guests from the company. Trudy's family plus a few of Woody's friends also came to about thirty people. The crowd was the perfect size for a luau. Sawhorse tables were set with checkered tablecloths. The sun was still hot and had a few hours before setting. The lake was calm, and torches kept the "no see-ems" and mosquitoes away. But far out on Lake Michigan giant thunderclouds were building up and seemed as if they would release their anvil-headed fury before the evening was over.

Trudy knew that she was doing what she had to be doing. She felt that she had no choice. Fate had doomed her to this marriage. She was calm and peaceful, as she looked at all the guests, when she climbed down from the carriage. She felt like Marie Antoinette stepping from her carriage on the way to the guillotine.

Later at dusk with the torches making an aisle, and the guests standing on either side, she walked by herself, giving herself away without the help of a father or uncle or any male. No one owned Trudy Mitchell, but now Woody would. Soon she would give up her identity, her persona to be co-opted, annexed, acquired as a man's wife losing her name, her freedom, and her right to decide her own destiny.

As she slowly walked down the sandy aisle on the northern Michigan beach with the sun dropping over the big lake between the thunderclouds, she looked at her future husband waiting for her. She was going to put her future and her life and her future children's lives into this fragile and human man's hands.

Trudy Mitchell, now almost Mrs. Ernest Barker Woodward III, had a strange thought. She remembered once reading that all of the movies of the thirties and forties ended in either marriage or death.

As she approached Woody, she thought, "Is there a difference?"

Chapter J

From a pamphlet about the Greensky Hill United Methodist Church

In the 1830's Peter Greensky, a Chippewa Indian, preached the gospel and converted his Indian brothers and sisters to Christianity. He served as a guide and interpreter for his fellow missionary and also acquired a following of his own as a strong preacher with great influence among his people. In 1860 he was put in charge of the all Indian Pine River Mission near Charlevoix, serving there until his death in 1866.

This simple log church was built at the mission in the 1840's. Surrounded by trees marking the site of a long sacred meeting place, the church was constructed with large hewn logs notched at the corners and laid horizontally over a stone foundation. Much of the lumber used in the building was brought by canoe from Traverse City.

For many years the mission was the scene of an annual camp meeting, which drew Indians from several states and Canada for revival meetings and a chance to renew personal and cultural ties. Today the church is used by an active racially mixed congregation, some of who are descendants of the original worshippers. Presently the church holds Sunday morning worship services, Sunday school, Bible Study, UMW meetings and fellowship gatherings. The church has recently completed its new fellowship hall. This building enables Greensky Hill to reach out to its community in new ways.

The Greensky Hill United Methodist Church is a Registered Michigan Historic site. This church is located in a beautiful wooded setting just five miles from Charlevoix on Old Highway 31.

Just beyond the winding dirt road to the church, on private land, eight crooked trees stand in a circle. They are known as the "Council Trees." It is told when the trees were twelve feet tall, the Indians used strips of basswood bark to bend the trees, making them grow crooked and thus undesirable to the lumbering white men.

Between the church and Susan Lake (located nearby) is a burial ground. Several hundred Native Americans are buried there. Many of the wooden grave markers have disintegrated and the names etched in cement on cobblestone markers have washed away with more than a century of rain and snowfall. Peter Greensky was buried in this cemetery, but the site in unknown.

The outdoor amphitheater is used for summer and camp meetings. Methodist services for the Indian congregation at Greensky Church are held regularly throughout the year. Visitors are always welcome.

*   *   *

From the *History of the Ottawa and Chippewa Indians of Michigan*, pp.21-23.

Perhaps the reader would like to know what became of those two persons who escaped from the lamented tribe Mishinemackinawgoes. I will here give it just as it is related in our traditions, although this may be considered, at this age, as a fictitious story; but every Ottawa and Chippewa to this day believes it to be positively so. It is related that the two persons escaped were two young people, male and female, and they were lovers. After everything got quieted down, they fixed their snowshoes inverted and crossed the lake on the ice, as snow was quite deep on the ice, and they went towards the north shore of Lake Huron. The object of inverting their snowshoes was that in case any person should happen

to come across their track on the ice, their
track would appear as if going towards the
island. They became so disgusted with human nature, it is related, that they shunned
every mortal being, and just lived by themselves, selecting the wildest part of the country. Therefore, the Ottawas and Chippewas
called them "Paw-gwa-tchaw-nish-naw-boy."
The last time they were seen by the Ottawas, they had ten children—all boys, and
all living and well. And every Ottawa and
Chippewa believes to this day that they are
still in existence and roaming in the wildest part of the land, but as supernatural beings—that is, they can be seen or unseen,
just as they see fit to be; and sometimes they
simply manifested themselves as being
present by throwing a club or a stone at a
person walking in a solitude, or by striking
a dog belonging to the person walking; and
sometimes by throwing a club at the lodge,
night or day, or hearing their footsteps walking around the wigwam when the Indians
would be camping out in an unsettled part
of the country, and the dogs would bark,
just as they would bark at any strange person approaching the door. And sometimes
they would be tracked on snow by hunters,
and if followed on the track, however recently passed, they never could be overtaken. Sometimes when an Indian would
be hunting or walking in solitude, he would
suddenly be seized with an unearthly fright,
terribly awe stricken, apprehending some
great evil. He feels very peculiar sensation

from head to foot—the hair of his head
standing and feeling stiff like a porcupine
quill. He feels almost benumbed with
fright, and yet he does not know what it is;
and looking in every direction to see something, but nothing to be seen which might
cause sensation of terror. Collecting himself, he would then say, "Pshaw! It's nothing
here to be afraid of. It's nobody else but
Paw-gwa-tchaw-nish-naw-boy is approaching
me. Perhaps he wanted something of me."
They would then leave something on their
tracks—tobacco, powder, or something else.
Once in a great while they would appear,
and approach the person to talk with him,
and in this case, it is said, they would always
begin with the sad story of their great catas-
trophe at the Island of Mackinac. And who-
ever would be so fortunate as to met and
see them and to talk with them, such person would always become a prophet to his
people, either Ottawa or Chippewa. Therefore, Ottawas and Chippewas called these
supernatural beings "Paw-gwa-tchaw-nish-
naw-boy," which is, strictly, "Wild roaming
supernatural being."

Pine river country, in Charlevoix
County, Michigan, when this country was all
wild, especially near Pine Lake, was once
considered as the most famous resort of
these kind of unnatural beings. I was once
conversing with one of the first white settlers of that portion of the country, who
settled near to the place now called Boyne
City, at the extreme end of the east arm of

Pine Lake (now Lake Charlevoix). In the conversation he told me that many times they had been frightened, particularly during the nights, by hearing what sounded like human footsteps around outside of their cabin; and their dog would be terrified, crouching at the doorway, snarling and growling, and sometimes fearfully barking. When daylight came, the old man would go out in order to discover what it was or if he could track anything around his cabin, but he never could discover a track of any kind. These remarkable, mischievous, audible, fanciful, appalling apprehensions were of very frequent occurrence before any other inhabitants or settlers came near to his place; but now, they do not have such apprehensions since many settlers came.

*   *   *

From the Charlevoix County Public Record—Recopied Record No. Charlevoix County

1918—Bolton, Prudence

Date of death—Feb. 15, 1918
Prudence Bolton
Female—Indian
Single
16/ months—5/weeks—3 days
Place of death—Charlevoix
Strychnine poisoning—suicidal
Birthplace—Michigan

Occupation—at home
Parents—Richard Bolton—MI.
Anna Topasash—MI.
Date of record—April 24, 1918

Richard Castle

Date of death—Feb. 15, 1918
Male/ white/ married
21/ place of death—Charlevoix
Strychnine poisoning
Birthplace—Michigan
Occupation—printer
Parents—Wm. Castle
Clara E. Davis
Residence—Ohio
Date of record—April 24, 1918

EPILOGUE

I am Crow Woman flying on the thermals above the big lake. I see all of the heartache and sorrow below me. The souls that are still bound on the earth by their desires and deeds will haunt the living among them.

Flying along the shore on Little Traverse Bay I follow the road inland that the Bacon family traveled in a horse and wagon with the teenage Hemingway boy. He thought that he was in love with Prudence then. Her ghost followed him his whole life. He never forgot his first love. She had wound her destiny into his brain and sinews and then ended her life.

This land still echoes with the anguished cries of the smallpox victims tricked by the British. The tortured sounds of the chiefs and children whisper in the pines and birches on the headlands of the former fifteen-mile long Odawa settlement of the "Land of the Crooked Tree." The pitiful cries of the last of passenger pigeons hunted to extinction by the white men on these same shores rise up with the

263

moaning gales off the huge freshwater sea called
Lake Michigan. The Windigo hunts in the winter
wastes, moving soundlessly on his search for prey .The
"wild roaming supernatural beings" called "Paw-gwa-
tchaw-nish-naw-boys" still make the hair stand up on
the back of necks of those in the woods of the land I
fly over.

Now on a descending flight I soar over little Susan
Lake lying in the shadow of the larger Lake
Charlevoix that is dwarfed by the earth-bending vista
of Lake Michigan to the west. My wings stretch black
against the winter sky, as I coast lower and lower over
the Greensky church in the forest near Susan Lake.
In this sacred grove of Native American people I hear
the cries from the unmarked graves.

I caw out messages of comfort and warnings from
the other Anishnabek. I drop berries and nuts for
the Feast of the Dead celebrated by the humans still
walking the earth. May the Great Manitou protect
you and someday carry your souls safely home to the
spirit world in the west in the region beyond the sky.

Printed in the United States
1276900001B/478-483